T0031003

SECOND EDITION—Updated and Expanded

Ten Things
Your Student
with Autism
Wishes You Knew

Ellen Notbohm

author of *Ten Things Every Child with*
Autism Wishes You Knew

Ten Things Your Student with Autism Wishes You Knew, Second Edition

All marketing and publishing rights guaranteed to and reserved by:

FUTURE HORIZONS INC.

(817) 277-0727
(817) 277-2270 (fax)
E-mail: info@fhautism.com
www.fhautism.com

© 2022 Ellen Notbohm
Website: https://ellennotbohm.com
Email: emailme@ellennotbohm.com
Social media: Facebook, Instagram, Twitter, LinkedIn, Pinterest

For foreign rights licensing, please contact the author at emailme@ellennotbohm.com

All rights reserved.
Printed in the USA.

No part of this publication may be reproduced in any manner whatsoever without the express written permission of the author.

ISBN: 9781949177862

Praise for
Ten Things Your Student with Autism Wishes You Knew, Second Edition

The two biggest take-home messages from this book are the importance of parents and teachers working together as a team and understanding that your autistic child thinks differently. *Ten Things Your Student with Autism Wishes You Knew* will help parents and teachers learn more effective methods for teaching children on the spectrum.

> — Temple Grandin, PhD, author of *The Way I See It* and *Thinking in Pictures*

*

It is a delight to find a book that creates a crack in the shell of autism, leading us to a better understanding of students with ASD. Ellen Notbohm offers us a glimpse of the inner thoughts of a child with this disorder, something that is often missed when teaching this student. A wonderful addition to any educator's library!

> — Sheila Wagner, M.Ed., author of the *Inclusive Programming for Elementary, Middle School and High School Students with Autism* book series

*

A breath of fresh air! Ellen Notbohm leaves behind reliance on tired, rigid systems of interventions and instead delves into vital transactional approaches that are so sorely needed.

The most important part of any IEP is not the diagnostic category but the individual's student profile. This book makes that often-neglected section come alive. For it is only by seeing the unique beauty in each child that change can happen. There is no place for cookie cutter formulae or reliance on specific treatment modalities. Autistic students learn differently and must be taught differently. Again, the book shows us how.

Further, when insisting that only the child should "change" in order to learn, we omit an essential ingredient. That is the role of the teacher in being able to change, innovate and accommodate in a transactional fashion. Hooray for circular learning!

Once we truly see each student with fresh eyes, understanding that their behaviors always have communicative intent, that kids do well if they can, that trust curiosity and respect are key, then we can break old, tired molds and instead allow the child's innate individuality to shine forth and succeed.

An essential book for any parent, educator, and developmental pediatrician!

— Raun D. Melmed, MD, FAAP, director of the Melmed Center and co-founder and medical director of the Southwest Autism Research and Resource Center, Phoenix AZ, PhD, LCSW and author of *Autism: Early Intervention, Autism and the Extended Family, Autism Parent Handbook: Beginning with the End Goal in Mind*, and the *ST4 Mindfulness Book for Kids* series

✳

In a sequel to her groundbreaking best-seller *Ten Things Every Child with Autism Wishes You Knew*, Ellen Notbohm brings the same intelligence, humanity, and compassionate clarity to educators that her earlier volume brought to parents. There are gems on every page, an impeccable blend of wisdom and heart.

Ten Things Your Student with Autism Wishes You Knew is an important book for adults who want to do right by the children entrusted to their care. In fact, Notbohm's framework of mutuality, attention, curiosity, and wholeness is something that will benefit all children who are struggling to be known and understood—to connect, feel that they matter, and find where they belong.

A brilliant volume that's sure to be another perennial best-seller, Notbohm's thoughtful and actionable must-have handbook is sure to expand the number of parents, teachers, and counselors who count on her work to guide them.

— Barbara Probst, PhD, LCSW and author of *When Labels Don't Fit*

It's always a joy and an education to read Ellen Notbohm's books, and her second edition of *Ten Things Your Student with Autism Wishes You Knew* is no exception. I love the book's underlying and over-arching themes of optimism, respect for differences, and belief in our students. We are reminded and encouraged to be curious about their unique learning styles, to foster their own curiosity as an important learning tool, and to learn from our students, so we can teach them in the ways they learn best. Most importantly, she shines a light on the joy that is an integral part of knowing and teaching these students. Ellen includes personal experiences, insights from teachers and other professionals, and authentic lived-experience viewpoint from autistic author Jennifer McIlwee Myers. The questions and prompts for discussion, self-reflection, or self-expression would be perfect for a teachers' book club, school autism training, or personal independent study. Although written with students on the autism spectrum in mind and heart, each of these Ten Things would be important for all students. There is just so much to love in this book!

— Wendela Whitcomb Marsh, MA, BCBA, RSD, author of *Recognizing Autism in Girls and Women, Independent Living with Autism: Your Roadmap to Success,* and *Autism Parent Handbook* with Raun Melmed, MD, FAAP

*

If you only read one book about autism, let this be the one. And prepare for emotional impact. Once again, drawing on firsthand experience and literature, Notbohm shares her gift of shining light, optimism, and profound wisdom in a conversational style that is both scholarly and uplifting. Notbohm never minces words about an obvious, vital truth—in order to help students reach their full potential, we must first understand the world as they experience it. With humor and heart, Notbohm offers clear insights and immediate strategies to help educators, parents, and other helpers to do just that. First, and foremost, Notbohm understands the power of the child's perspective by showing us how to improve the way we listen, how to better demonstrate respect, and develop trust to believe what we are being told. An absorbing, enormously instructive book that I couldn't put down.

— Debra Whiting Alexander, PhD, LMFT, post-trauma treatment specialist, Former Associate Professor of Psychology and School Counseling, Bushnell University, and former Adjunct Professor of Psychology at Oregon State University. Author of *Children Changed by Trauma* and *A River for Gemma*

*

Ten Things Your Student with Autism Wishes You Knew combines wisdom from a student with autism, his family, and his educators throughout the continuum of their school years from pre-school to higher education, delivered through analogies, metaphors, and hard facts. It is written with humor and easy-to-remember phrases so the reader can learn to hear the voices of our autistic students and respond in ways that are meaningful to them. The book starts with clear succinct points that lay out a guide map, then clarifies the essential information to help teachers offer their best work for their students' growth. Through numerous and invaluable examples, Ten Things provides insight that can be used to generalize an understanding of the VERY different way the brain of a person with autism is wired.

The Ten Things laid out in this book are critical to teaching students with ASD. But you'll find much that benefits all children as well. Recalling my own 40-year career as a teacher, a learning specialist, and a district supervisor of special education teachers, I highly recommend *Ten Things Your Student with Autism Wishes You Knew* for your educational resource library.

— Eileen Harrison Sanchez, MEd, LDTC, NCED-R, PreK-12 Special Education Supervisor (retired), Princeton Public Schools, New Jersey, and author of *Freedom Lessons*

*

Ellen Notbohm has done it again! Every educator should own and frequently refer to this book. Every parent of a child with autism should give a copy of this book to each of their student's teachers. The communication strategies in Chapter 2 can be life-changing not only for a child, but also for the adults in that child's life. As both a parent and an educator, I recommend this book for the impact it can have not only on a child's school year, but also on their life.

— Bobbi Reilly Sheahan, substitute teacher, homeschool teacher, and author of *What I Wish I'd Known About Raising a Child With Autism*

*

Ten Things Your Student with Autism Wishes You Knew is an essential guidebook for anyone who loves, works with, and advocates for children.

One of the biggest challenges for students with different learning needs is when those who are supposed to be supporting them do not understand how their minds and bodies interact with others and their world. Understanding how the individual on the autism spectrum connects with the world and being willing to accommodate a way of interacting that differs from your own is vital to building the foundation for positive relationships, instruction, advocacy, and equity. This book is an in-depth primer to understanding the most prominent common threads that run through the autism community.

Ellen Notbohm's advocacy is informed by experience, research, empathy and a passion for making the lives of spectrum individuals and those who interact with them more fulfilling. This book provides clear and specific guidance that is doable, logical, meaningful and relevant. It should be required reading for all child centered professionals.

— Kassie Evans Halpin, M.Ed, Special Educator, Service Learning Coordinator, Advocate for Educational Diversity, Equity, Inclusion, and Individualized Support

Also by Ellen Notbohm

Nonfiction

Ten Things Every Child with Autism Wishes You Knew, Third Edition

1001 Great Ideas for Teaching and Raising Children with Autism or Asperger's, Second Edition with co-author Veronica Zysk

The Autism Trail Guide: Postcards from the Road Less Traveled

Fiction

The River by Starlight

For Connor and Bryce

... as if my books could be anything but

Contents

A note on language usage in this book

Vocabulary and language usage among both autistic and non-autistic people have evolved over the last several decades, and it will continue evolving to reflect growing knowledge, differences in cultures, and individual preferences. No single format can represent all.

This book uses the terms *autistic*, *with autism*, *with ASD* (autism spectrum disorder), and *on the spectrum* interchangeably.

This book recognizes all gender preferences. He/him, she/her, and the singular they/them are used interchangeably.

Preface

In the spring of 2004, I wrote a short piece called "Ten Things Every Child with Autism Wishes You Knew." I did it on a semi-dare. While gathering ideas for our book *1001 Great Ideas for Teaching and Raising Children with Autism or Asperger's*, my co-author and editor Veronica Zysk sent me a wish list article written by a mother to a teacher. I'd seen other such articles, and I'd seen articles written from a teacher's point of view, but I had never seen anything that portrayed an autistic child's point of view. "But who speaks for the child?" I commented to Veronica.

"You do," came the reply. "Write that piece."

The words that brought those original ten things to life flowed out of me freely, as if coming from some natural part of the landscape. Never could I have imagined the response. It traveled the internet like brush fire and hit print in dozens of publications on every continent (okay, not Antarctica). Within the year, a book based on the article followed, and it too brought new friends to me from around the world.

When I started getting requests for more articles of a similar nature, I had to ponder what it was about *Ten Things* that resonated so deeply among such a diverse group of people. It seemed to erase all borders—gender, cultural, racial, political, religious, economic. Readers made it clear that the resonance came from the fact that it spoke with a child's voice, a voice not heard often enough and, in many cultures and communities, not at all. For those voices to go unheeded is sad and wrong but not surprising when one of the hallmarks of autism is its veritable steeplechase of obstacles to effective communication.

There was, and still is, great need and ever-increasing willingness to understand the world as autistic children experience it. So the voice of our child returned in a second article, "Ten Things Your Student with Autism Wishes You Knew," to tell us what children on the autism spectrum wish their teachers knew. It too became a torch passed from reader to reader around the world. It was only a matter of time until my publisher and editor both suggested—firmly—that this book was a next step both natural and necessary. At the same time, teachers from preschool through university contacted me, wanting to use my work as training materials for family members, caregivers, administrators, and staff. The child's voice provided a compelling starting point for easing a general population into the shift in thinking that is necessary if we're to succeed in reaching and teaching our autistic children.

This book happened for two overarching reasons. The first is that, from the moment I heard the word "autism" applied to my son Bryce, I was determined to play the hand our family had been dealt without bitterness and without blame in as constructive, positive, and healthy a manner as we could. The second reason is that, although I had already (obviously) signed on for my role as a parent, I realized quickly that I would need to wear a teacher's hat for far more than table manners and tying shoelaces. I would have to teach things I didn't know yet, and I would have to teach them in a manner that wasn't the slightest bit familiar to me. In other words, I would have to be a learner first before I could be a teacher.

> **I would have to teach things I didn't know yet, and in a manner that wasn't the slightest bit familiar to me. I would have to be learner first, before I could be a teacher.**

This is the dangerous juncture at which, whether *teacher* means educator or parent/caregiver, it's easy to become overwhelmed.

There's so much about autism we don't know or understand! There's so much this child needs to learn! There are only six hours in the school day! There are only 175 days in a school year! There are only fifteen (or less!) years left until he's an adult! Yes, I needed to become a learner first, but the first thing I needed to learn was how to pace myself and pace the journey. I couldn't and didn't need to know everything up front. I could and would learn as we went along. I only needed to know enough to stay one step ahead of my son, within beckoning distance. And when even that modest pace wasn't possible, I became comfortable learning alongside him, the same things at the same time, which had its own kind of lovely power. Equally important was learning that I couldn't go this alone—and that I wouldn't have to. Although Bryce would be my primary teacher, all sorts of others, children and adults, would have a hand in teaching me as well.

What is it about any teacher that incites learning, makes us curious about our world? Aren't we all more open to learning when we trust the messenger and feel that both our efforts and our personal way of thinking and doing are respected? If we feel validated by our teachers as individual selves, we're more willing to take the risks necessary to learning. Don't we all respond more eagerly to those who actively believe in us—as opposed to those who communicate impatience, indifference, doubt, or resignation?

It's not often easy, but it works. And it worked for my son because he—and my whole family—had the immeasurable advantage of learning from immensely talented and caring teachers every step of the way. But I can't emphasize this more strongly: we weren't "lucky." I looked at dozens of schools within the twenty-five-mile radius surrounding our home until I found the one that stood out as being the right fit for both our sons (the older having been diagnosed with ADHD). We took rigorous steps to get them into that school. What those steps were isn't as important as the fact that we were willing to do whatever it took (to the extent our personal conditions allowed), because the culture of the teaching community at that school was what our sons needed to succeed. What I learned alongside the many dedicated teachers who've worked with Bryce was the impetus for this book. Their voices ring throughout, whether identified or not.

My search for the right school narrowed down to The One as I interviewed the last of the neighborhood parents and professionals on my list. Eerily, I'd been hearing the same remark over and over: "Oh yes, it's a wonderful school. But whatever you do, when you get to third grade, make sure you get Jackie, the teacher to end all teachers!" I found out that Jackie Druck had this reputation going back several decades. When Bryce did get assigned to Jackie for third grade, I spent as much time in the classroom as he would allow (respecting that this was his world and he didn't want me there more than occasionally, a fully understandable piece of his growing independence). And in my time spent in Jackie's classroom, I became enormously baffled. For such a grandiose reputation, she was a low-key, unassuming person. Her classroom was calm and orderly, the peaceful, fluid music of Enya often playing softly. I could not for the life of me put my finger on any specific thing she was doing that kept two generations of kids, including Bryce, so spellbound.

And yet.

When the kids wrote their year-end essays highlighting their favorite parts of third grade, it was clear that most, if not all, were simply in love with her. When she retired shortly thereafter, the party had to be held in a *city park* to accommodate all who wanted to come.

I had to mull over all this with my old college girlfriend Shirley, a nationally board-certified teacher. Shirley and Jackie had never had any kind of contact, and yet Shirley didn't hesitate to answer my question. "I can tell you what it is," she said. "I'd be willing to bet she has a deep, inherent respect for each child and that she communicates that to them. Children are willing to do quite a bit for teachers who first and foremost respect them as individuals."

Two telling exchanges unfolded at the beginning of our year in Jackie's classroom. At our first meeting, she told me she was excited to work with Bryce. She said she'd taught only one other student with autism a few years earlier, and he'd been quite different from Bryce. I had to smile a little as I gently told her that if she'd been teaching for thirty-five years, she'd had far more than one. But she may not have known what she was looking at. Sure enough, a few weeks later I got a call. "You're right," she said. "I've had dozens of them. *How much more I could have done if I had known.*"

Jackie's willingness to be a lifelong learner, her curiosity, her respect for all manner of learners was indeed the key to her success. At parent conferences two months into the school year, she greeted me with, "I'm going to have to keep him for a couple of years."

I was stunned. I had thought things were going so well. "Is he doing that poorly?" I asked.

"No, silly," she said. "I'm just that intrigued by him. There's so much more I need to learn about him. From him."

Before we begin

While this book contains some specific suggestions for the classroom, its primary purpose is to fold those kinds of ideas into the larger concepts that, hopefully, govern the teacher in all of us, whether trained educator, support staff, parent, therapist, administrator, family member—or Quidditch coach! If you're familiar with the Harry Potter saga, I'm sure you noticed that the Quidditch teams have no adult coaches. They're completely student-led units, left to win or lose on their own experiences, knowledge, and ability to work as a team, with no adult guidance. Perhaps that's why they call it magic?

Strategies and tactics are vital and necessary, the nuts and bolts of the educational quest. But we want to go beyond that, to consider how smoothly the whole locomotive will chug after all the bolts are in place, after adding the correct formulation of fuel that will enable it to move. A former in-law of mine headed up the aircraft maintenance operation at a military base. He summed up this critical job as "tightening up the loose stuff and loosening up the tight stuff." And so it is with fine-tuning a whole child to their highest potential. Their future success is predicated on much more than any facts we attempt to teach them.

To be able to hear the voices of our autistic students and respond in ways that are meaningful to them, we must be able to step outside our own deeply ingrained perspectives and frame of reference. Most of us think in words, while this child may think in pictures. We embrace the nuances of language, while they need concrete explanations. While we infer context and motivation from our observations of others, they may be "mindblind" to such social subtleties. What smells good to us makes an autistic child nauseous. Sounds that we routinely filter out make their heads pound. Some adults doggedly insist the autistic child is "off in their own little world" and must "join the real world," but we must start with accepting and acting from an understanding that the child's own world is as real to them as ours is to us. We encourage and motivate our child to join a larger world, not through insults, shaming, and narrow perspectives, but by giving them goals that are clear, relevant, incremental, developmentally appropriate, and attainable, and then giving them the tools, problem-solving strategies, and emotional support to achieve those goals. We teach them how to reach for realistic achievements and qualities, and we adjust the goals to reflect their progress and the constant change around them. That's the real real world we should want for them.

Nearly every teacher with whom I've spent time tells me that real-world magic lies in "seeing the light bulb go on" with any child. If you can't find the switch, the groping can get frustrating. My hope is that this book will guide your hand to that switch. It's at the same time easier than you think and more challenging than you think.

Much of this book will involve exploring the ways in which your autistic students experience their social and physical landscape differently—in the way they think, relate to others, and process sensory input. But as teachers and parent-teachers, we must never lose sight of the fact that autistic children share many characteristics with non-autistic children. The Ten Things laid out in this book are critical to teaching children with ASD. But you'll find much that benefits all children as well. *Please* note that I say "all children," not "normal children."

You won't see the word "normal" in this book outside quotation marks. As many parents have experienced, my child's autism diagnosis provoked others to ask variations of the question, "Will he ever learn to be normal?" The first few times I heard such presumptuous and insensitive questions stupefied me. But later I found them so sadly lacking in human perspective that I almost came to pity the asker. I would smile and wink and breeze by it with "If ever there comes a time that there is such a thing!" or "Naw, he'll never be a washer-dryer setting." And I would quote Canadian songwriter Bruce Cockburn, who nailed it: "The trouble with normal is it always gets worse."

A generation of autistic children have grown into articulate and outspoken autistic adults in the years since the original edition of this book was published. Many have made it clear that not only was "normal" not accessible to them, it's not something they aspire to, and in some contexts, it's not healthy for them. As author, autism advocate, and self-described "Aspie-at-Large" Jennifer McIlwee Myers tells us later in the book, "Please don't try to make us 'normal.' We'd much rather be functional. It's hard to be functional when you have to spend all your time and energy focusing on not tapping your feet."

The COVID-19 pandemic that began in 2020 flung "normal" to the prevailing winds of all physical, social, and emotional latitudes again and again. Buzz phrases like "the new normal" and "back to normal" and "a return to normalcy" seemed to defy definition, shape-shifting from day to day, month to month, person to person, and just about every other variable. The disability community raised an I-told-ya-so collective eyebrow, having long rejected the term "normal" as being undefinable in any meaningful way. As Myers described it: "Disabled people are very used to limited socio-economic clout, especially with health care, so a lot of what's happening is just their/our norm, but more intense. Can't get things you need just to function? Can't get medical care you need because your need doesn't count right now? Can't leave the house without risk and difficulty? Par for the course for a lot of disabled folks."

So, what is "normal," and how does it, how should it, impact how we teach autistic children? My best definition of normal, the one I've carried with me daily for many years, the one that offers us open-ended opportunity, came from—of course!—an educator.

"A Word about Normal" is my one of my favorite passages from any of my books. In it, a middle school speech therapist answers a mother's concern that her son hasn't made many friends and might not "do all the normal teen things we did."

> "When your son came to me last year," the speech therapist tells Mom, "his social thinking skills were almost nonexistent. He didn't understand why he should say hi to people in the halls, he didn't know how to ask a question to further a conversation, or how to engage with a peer during the lunch hour. Now he's working on those things. That's a huge amount of progress."

> "But he's only made two friends."

> "I would rephrase that: he's made two friends! One shares his interest in model trains and one shares his interest in running. He knows how you feel, though. So I am going to share with you what he told me the other day. He said, 'I don't want a lot of friends. I can't handle a lot of friends. More than one at a time stresses me out. I can talk to these two friends about things I'm interested in. They are great for me.'

> "Walk through this or any other school," the SLP continues. "You'll see a huge range of 'normal' middle school behavior. You'll see nerdy

normal, sporty normal, musical normal, artsy normal, techie normal. Kids tend to gravitate to groups that make them feel safe. For now, your son has found his group. You and I walk a fine line: honoring his choices while continuing to teach him the skills he needs to feel comfortable expanding his boundaries."

Your child has many social selves. To embrace all of them, and therefore him as a whole child, is to redefine how we view "normal"—one person at a time.

[excerpted from *1001 Great Ideas for Teaching and Raising Children with Autism or Asperger's*, second edition, by Ellen Notbohm and Veronica Zysk (2010, Future Horizons)]

In the end, it's not about singling out the child on the spectrum for "special treatment." It's about teaching to the strengths and needs of a different kind of learner. Progress *will* come. You'll see the light bulb click on (albeit in perhaps unpredictable increments), and the results will be exciting. Isn't that why you became a teacher in the first place?

Let's get started.

Here are ten things your student with autism

wishes you knew

Learning Is Circular

We're all both teachers and students.

Some of my teachers have said they've learned a lot from me. This helped me see that learning flows in all directions, not only from you as the teacher to me as the student, but from student to teacher, from student to student, from teacher to teacher, from teacher to parent, and from parent to teacher. This big circle of learning makes it work for all of us. Think of what happens when teachers can only think on a one-way street. There's a scene in a very funny movie called *Ferris Bueller's Day Off*. A kid is asleep with his head on the desk in a puddle of drool while the teacher drones on and on, trying to get "Anyone? Anyone?" to respond. I'm pretty sure that student's not learning anything.

You might tell me that the world is like a double-sided 2,000-piece jigsaw puzzle of learning opportunities. But my autism can make it difficult for me to recognize those opportunities. I don't learn in ways most people do. My autism way of thinking can interfere with my ability to understand the information that surrounds me. But here's one thing I do know: you have as much to learn from me as I do from you.

Autistic students need teachers who love being learners, too. You will help me learn things I need to know, and what you learn from me is very important, too—because there are lots more like me headed your way.

We're a Team

Success depends on all of us working together.

I usually think of "team" as a sports word. The players play their own positions but they wear the same clothes so everyone can easily see that they're all working together. Each player is important and the team members depend on each other. They share their wins and their losses together, slap high-fives when one of them does something great. They help each other out when one of them is having a bad day.

I looked up the word "team" in the dictionary, and I think we should all tape this definition on our bathroom mirrors: "team: a group of people who share a purpose or task and depend on each other over an extended period of time to succeed." I may or may not be good at sports, but as an autistic child, having people around me who want to play on *my* team is what I need to succeed, and nothing less.

I Think Differently

Teach me in a way that's meaningful to *me*.

Because I think differently, my autism requires that you teach differently. If you want to teach me to see life and learning as a range of colors, you have to start by understanding that through my eyes, many of life's experiences are black and white, all or nothing.

Autism is a different way of *thinking*. My brain works differently than yours. It's not weird or wrong—just different. Yet your way of thinking is so natural to you that you can't even imagine that *it might be foreign to me*.

For you, the associations between the things you learn, the things that happen to you, and the people around you form naturally and without someone specifically teaching you. For me, all of these parts exist in independent, unrelated cells, and I struggle to connect the dots. Each dot stands alone.

Please realize how deeply this different way of thinking affects learning, and teach me in a manner that respects how I think, who I am, and what I am—a child with autism.

Behavior Is Communication: Yours, Mine, and Ours

I hear adults talk about misbehavior, bad behavior, negative behavior, behavior that comes "out of nowhere" or "for no reason." To me, *all* behavior is just behavior, and all my behavior has a reason. It's information about what's happening between you and me, about what's happening inside of me, and about how factors we can or can't see in our environment affect me. It tells you, when my words can't—or when no one is listening—how I'm experiencing what's happening around me. When you try to change my behavior without finding the what, the why, or the who behind it, I notice that everyone's behavior changes—for the worse!

Start by believing this: I do want to learn to interact appropriately. What you call negative behavior interferes with my learning, and no child wants or likes to get our feelings crushed by the reactions we get to our "bad" behavior. Such behavior usually means one or more of my senses or emotions has gone into overload, or I can't communicate my wants or needs, or I don't understand what's expected of me. Or I do understand what's expected but don't have the skills or knowledge (even if you think I do), and I dread the "bad behavior" I get from others when I fail.

9

Behavior is a symptom. Look beyond the behavior to find the source of my discomfort. Merely getting me to stop these behaviors isn't enough; it doesn't address the basic cause or need, so I'll likely come up with another behavior to try to meet my need. Identify that need—then alleviate the source and teach me acceptable (to both of us) ways to cope so that real learning can flow.

Glitched, Garbled, and Bewildered

If we can't communicate,
neither of us will learn much.

Teach the Whole Me

I'm much more than a set of broken or missing parts.

I'm a kid. When I look in the mirror, that's what I see—a kid, not those words I hear, like "issues" or "symptoms." Like you, I'm a one-of-a-kind combination of body, mind, and spirit. Like you, I have a unique personality with my own ideas, interests, likes and dislikes, dreams and fears.

Teach *me*, a whole child and future adult, not a collection of symptoms or missing skills, or a set of broken or disconnected pieces. Teach me not just what to do, but how all the parts of me, like my thoughts and feelings and reactions, have to work together for me to understand and be comfortable in the world of "we" and not just "me." Feeding me facts or skills with no social or emotional connection between them may not be teaching me much at all.

Be Curious

...be *very* curious.

When I was learning to read, my speech therapist would "picture walk" through books with me. On each page, we would look at the picture and say, "I wonder." I wonder what will happen next? I wonder why this person looks sad? I wonder who's knocking at the door? Together we would find answers to all of our "I wonder" questions.

Be curious about what makes me tick and about the back roads you may have to travel to reach me. Like many autistic children, my need for routine and familiarity means I may not be naturally curious, so I need you to be doubly so. Your curiosity shows me wonderful things: that you care about me, and that beyond memorization and repetition, beyond what I need to do to just get by, real learning will happen only when I finally feel able to move out of my comfort space and into a world that's frequently fearful and overwhelming to me. And most importantly, I'll learn about the interesting and enjoyable experiences I can have if I can allow myself to be curious.

I wonder: how much can we learn together if we can remember to be curious?

Can I Trust You?

Build my trust in you, because only if I can trust you will learning unfold freely. Just because you're an adult in charge of me doesn't mean I'll automatically trust you. I may comply with your instructions, but that's not the same as trust, and compliance doesn't mean I'm learning either. I will trust someone who stays consistent, respects my individual needs, and does their best to meet them, and I will trust someone who's honest with me, even when—especially when—they don't know all the answers.

When I can trust you, I can more easily see that what you're trying to teach me is relevant and helpful to me (it is, isn't it?). When I can trust you, I can learn to trust myself. And when I can trust myself, just watch me learn!

Believe

That car guy Henry Ford said, "Whether you think you can or think you can't, you're right."

Believe that I can learn. Adapt your teaching to my needs and watch my learning grow and thrive.

Believe that you can make a difference for me and you will.

But before I understand that you believe *in* me, I need you to believe me. Believe me when I tell you something; however odd it sounds, be curious enough to probe. And if I can't find the right words, believe what my behavior tells you. I may not be as articulate as my peers, or I may not speak up because I've become used to people belittling, scolding, denying, or mocking what I say rather than believing me.

If you want to encourage me to be everything I can be, start by believing me. Then believe *in* me so I can stay the course long after I've left your classroom.

Teach Me "How to Fish"

See me as a capable adult and hold that vision.

The Chinese have a saying: "Give a man a fish and you feed him for a day. Teach a man to fish and you feed him for a lifetime." The most important things you can teach me won't be found in a book, on a worksheet, or in an app. I need to learn skills to live my adult life as independently and meaningfully as possible.

Make learning relevant for me. Teach me how to use knowledge in ways I'll need to use it to live as an adult who's able to take care of myself but also able to interact well with coworkers, neighbors, friends, and people of the world in general.

I once heard a fisherman describe fishing as the art of casting out the line and the science of reeling in the catch. Teach me both the art and science of my life.

Chapter One

Learning Is Circular

We're all both teachers and students.

The notion that learning is circular is neither new nor unique. Many of Bryce's teachers told me they learned a great deal from him and that they learn continually from all the children they teach. This seems not only natural to me, but exhilarating.

Yet I remember one mom, in the early days after my son's diagnosis, who bridled at these kinds of remarks. "I'm so tired of hearing teachers say they've learned so much from my kid! I want them to teach him, not learn from him." Reading between her lines, I heard an anxious urgency, the vastness of all she felt her son needed to learn colliding with the finite limitations of a six-hour school day. For parents and teachers alike (and the many who are both), we've all been frequent visitors to that impatient place, but we need to be ever-aware that it's counterproductive. In the classroom, in the home, and in the community, parents and teachers must, to the greatest extent we can, take advantage of learning opportunities as they present themselves. Passing up those opportunities in the name of saving time will eventually only slow the teaching process. How could it be otherwise?

Because I've learned side by side with so many outstanding teachers over the years, I've lived the power of circular learning in action, where teaching and learning energies zoom the circuits back and forth between all individuals of all ages and all stations in education and in life. It started right at the beginning, when Bryce entered preschool. The very gifted "Teacher Christine" Hunt personified circular learning. Before our year together was out, she was insisting that I write a book. Then she romped on me for seven years until I did.

No less a teacher was Veda Nomura, the occupational therapist who was part of Bryce's team of teachers. Veda patiently guided not just Bryce but me as well to understanding the devilishly complicated landscape of sensory integration. It was one of the toughest propositions I ever confronted in my life. When I finally succeeded, I had Veda on a pedestal so high as to induce vertigo.

So I was particularly smitten with Veda's contribution to a wall display in Teacher Christine's classroom. Each child and adult had contributed a photo of themselves, with a caption that filled in the phrase "I am learning to _____." Bryce wrote that he was learning to ride a training-wheel bike. Veda wrote: "I'm learning to raise teenagers." Her statement brought home to me that no matter how knowledgeable and capable any one of us may seem, we're all still learning, still searching for the best way to handle new challenges.

Many books, articles, and posts about autism refer to its "mystery," but I don't like that word. I'm not interested in whodunit. I want to know what comes next. And because I want to know what comes next, I don't like the implication of the word "mystery" if it suggests that "unknown" is synonymous with "unknowable." Just as a good mystery dissolves in the hands of a good detective, autism is knowable. We start by knowing that children with autism aren't a monolithic population. No two are exactly alike, and no single approach is a sure thing. Achieving success with an autistic child is often a matter of discovering what doesn't work as much as discovering what does, and either discovery may come to light with something as simple (and yet complex) as reframing or juxtapositioning our questions. It can be exhausting and exasperating, but never does it constitute failure. "Results!" Thomas Edison said. "Why, man, I have gotten a lot of results. I know several thousand things that won't work." In this same frame of mind, many parents and teachers, stymied by an autistic child's inability to express what they need but determined to find an inroad, finally made that successful connection with the child by asking the usual what-do-you-want? question in reverse—what do you *not* want, what do you *not* like, what should I *not* do? Reversing the perspective reversed the mystery.

German philosopher Martin Heidegger tells us, "Teaching is more difficult than learning because what teaching calls for is this: to let learn." That's an explosive, double-barreled concept, but it's the absolute embodiment of circular learning. As adults, we bear the burden. We must relinquish all our conceits and presumptions to let ourselves learn what we need to know to be able to teach an autistic child, whose thoughts originate in a thinking and processing architecture and frame of reference distinctly dissimilar to our own. Venturing into a place where we don't know the lay of the land and don't have all the answers can be intimidating, no question. "If, as a teacher you find that an uncomfortable place to be, I get it," says your autistic student. "That's how I feel quite a lot of the time, when so often I don't know the answers." This holds true for professionals and parents. But it's not a reason to not go there or not set the example of exploring our abilities and boundaries. A friend of ours once left a comfortable teaching job at a so-called nice school to take a job across town as assistant principal at a so-called tough school. When we asked him why, he said he considered it "an acceptable challenge." Discomfort can be a good thing when we embrace it as impetus to squirm to the next level of growth, at any age.

And then, when we have let ourselves learn well, we need to let our student learn. By its nature, this cannot be a pain-free process for us or for the child. The best among us will question whether we got it right, whether or what we could have done better. Did we hurt the child, who already struggles so because of their autism, unintentionally and/or needlessly?

I can still scarcely bear to think about all the mistakes I made with my son during those early stages of learning—from him, not from books—about his autism. But for all the times I berated myself mercilessly, there was a teacher on the other end of the phone saying, "This happens to all of us, Ellen. As parents and as teachers. He will forgive you if you forgive yourself."

Bryce and I both learned to push the boundaries of our resilience, and we learned from each other. Freely admitting my mistakes to him was a powerful learning tool. No one's infallible, and increasingly it struck me as odd that we require children to respect authority without considering that they might respect us more if we were honest about our humanity, to stop seeing that respect as an entitlement, but to require ourselves to earn our child's respect, every day. I never hesitated (and still don't) to apologize to my children when I was wrong. Whether it's because I misjudged, was careless, didn't have the right information, or simply should have known better, it was and still is more meaningful for them to pull them into the circle of life-learning where we can approach mistakes with curiosity rather than self-flagellation and say, "Whoa! That didn't work. I wonder what we could try next?" or "We learned something from that, didn't we? We'll know better what to do next time."

Our autistic student relies on us, the adults in his life, to learn about him from each other, too. Reading through my mailbox can be poignant. Parents tell me how much they have to share with their child's educators about his autism, if only the educators would listen and respect a parent's wisdom born of experience. Educators lament parents who resist, reject, disbelieve, and deny their professional observations and suggestions, even those based on what they learn from experience with the child during the school day.

Circular learning challenges us to lay aside our egos, preconceptions, and ingrained perspectives to become child-centered in our approach, to embrace the process as much as outcome, and to have the courage and confidence to step outside the lane lines, to willingly bump down a road less traveled. It challenges us to place less value on test scores and the top-down approach, and instead turn our efforts toward relationship-building, collaboration, and reigniting the thrill of exploration. Circular learning acknowledges that true teaching isn't about putting information into the minds of our students; rather, it's *striving to bring something out of every learner*. That learner isn't just the student; it's you, and me, and everyone with whom they will interact.

> **Circular learning is *striving to bring something out of every learner*. That learner isn't just the student; it's you, and me, and everyone with whom they will interact.**

From Day One, I accepted that I had to be a full partner and fellow learner in Bryce's education. I knew intuitively that my mission was to prepare him to live to the greatest degree possible as a capable, independent adult. And yet when a child is so young and the obstacles thrown up by autism seem so threatening, it's only natural that we cling to lifeboats who come along in the form of wise and effective teachers. One such person for me was Nola Shirley, one of Bryce's first paraeducators. More than one teacher referred to her as a miracle worker, and we'll hear more about her secret of success later in the book. For now, we step into her circle of learning at the parent-as-learner stop.

Far from limiting herself to teaching only Bryce, she played a major role in teaching me, a parent, about independence too. She had seen Bryce through three years of early education before judging, reluctantly, that he'd become too dependent upon her, and it was time to step away. In hindsight I'm forced to wonder if it was Bryce who'd become too dependent upon her—or me. I can still feel the sickening lurch my stomach took when, at the end of their last year together, I opened her note that read: "What a wonderful year we've had. I will not be working with Bryce in the next grade. I hope that the friendships we've forged in the last few years can last a lifetime." Later she told me she knew it was time to step away when she realized that he would look to her automatically, even for tasks of which he was well capable.

In this regard, it's clear that Bryce was more teachable than I was. He moved on to become ever more independent while I, for more than a decade after our first hello, still scurried back to Nola for answers, especially when I already knew the answer but didn't like it. She was my educator too, for the rest of her life. One year she sat next to me at a very special birthday party— mine, hosted by Teacher Christine, Teacher Veda, and other friends from that first preschool team. None of us could imagine going through the previous decade without the exchange of insights, experiences, and support that traveled our continuous loop. "We need you too," Veda had told me. "When kids leave us and move on, we almost never hear from parents, don't know what happens to the children, how we did, whether what we do works, or what we might have done better."

Disney's movie *Pocahontas* eloquently made the case for circular learning in the popular song "The Colors of the Wind." Pocahontas tells John Smith, "We are all connected to each other in a circle...that never ends." She admonishes him for being unable to value people who don't "think like you":

> But if you walk the footsteps of a stranger,
> You'll learn things you never knew you never knew.

If as teachers we're ever to feel comfortable and confident with autism, recognizing the teacher that lies within each of our students is the foundation of any success we'll achieve. It speaks to trust, respect, and the value of every individual, building blocks without which meaningful learning cannot flourish. The first step down that road is the wonderfully empowering acceptance of the fact that every moment is a teaching and learning moment, sometimes simply in just *being* as much as *doing*, and that we're all both teachers and students. It's an invitation to a dynamic partnership and to create multi-dimensional spheres of learning for all of us, but especially for our autistic students.

Step into the circle. They're counting on you. They want you to succeed.

Chapter Two

We're a Team

Success depends on all of us working together.

Just as it takes a village to raise a child, it takes a team to educate a child with autism. And just as nature does, education should abhor a vacuum. Teachers don't teach in a vacuum, parents don't rear their children in a vacuum, children don't develop in any significant way in a vacuum. That goes double for an autistic child, whose many social, sensory, and communication challenges may make that vacuum look like a mighty comfortable place. Strong team dynamics are essential if we're to succeed with our student over the span of his education years and into meaningful adulthood.

At the beginning of our odyssey, I had the painful but timely experience of seeing poor teamwork in action. Bryce had been placed in an early intervention preschool classroom conveniently housed at our neighborhood school. Children with various social communication difficulties (autism, Asperger's syndrome, ADHD, brain injury) made up half the class; neighborhood peers completed the group. Basing this region-wide class in our neighborhood school was fortuitous—it would give us a glimpse into what the school would be like for Bryce when he reached kindergarten age the following year.

I was out the metaphorical door of that school the instant I heard that a primary grade teacher had asked one of my son's paraeducators, with dripping sarcasm, "And what exactly is it you expect to accomplish with these kids?" Even if that particular staffer was the only one in the building giving off those kind of noxious fumes—and I considered it unlikely, given trickle-down thinking—it still meant that everyone around her was breathing them. I looked around the rest of the school. I saw a tired principal plodding through the last year or two before retirement. I saw a teaching staff with low morale, first grade classrooms with thirty-two kids, endemic behavior problems not being addressed. My search for a healthier environment was on.

We ended up at Capitol Hill School, whose culture reflected, blindingly, the worth and importance of all learners. The principal filled empty classrooms with special-needs preschool programs. The school didn't have a soccer team or orchestra but instead used discretionary funds for a full-time child development specialist, who provided everything from individual counseling to small group discussions to whole-class lessons on social dynamics. The resource/learning center was located in the hub of the school, not some out-of-the-way corner, and so many kids landed there for help that no stigma was ever attached. The school loudly trumpeted its status as a "No Put-Down Zone" and dealt with incidences of unkindness in any form speedily and firmly. The school reverberated with the spirit of teamwork.

Bryce attended Capitol Hill for seven years. He received services that increased as needed with each passing year. His teachers loved him to bits, and the principal defended him fiercely when necessary.

He progressed gracefully, each year beginning with virtually no regression and with enthusiasm bred of the comfort of familiarity. With the finesse of an Olympic relay team, he was handed off from each grade to the next by teachers who understood the importance of sharing their insights. All the mutual enthusiasm was infectious and produced big results.

As adults, we have to beware of straying too far from that bathroom mirror definition of "team" as a group of people whose success at their shared task demands interdependence of effort. Allowing ourselves to drift beyond planning sound moves and strategies into the politics, the personality clashes, the finger-pointing, the he said/she said/they said, the immovable preconceived assumption meeting the irresistible unsubstantiated stereotype—none of this is good team dynamics. Your student needs an *effective* multi-disciplinary team.

In our ever-evolving circle of learning, the components of team dynamics are simple:

- The actions we display to each other

- The attitudes we display to each other

These components come in three flavors: productive, indifferent, or poisonous. Each of us has the power to make the choice among those three. For our autistic students and their teachers, be they parent or educator, choosing to be a productive team player is a make-or-break-this-child choice.

What makes for productive team dynamics? Good team dynamics are a set of ground rules that all parties embrace because they know that the whole is more than the sum of all parts. Were this not true, we could make a human being by swishing thirty-five liters of water, twenty kilograms of carbon, and four liters of ammonia with the proper quantities of lime, phosphorus, salt, sulfur, iron, silicon, and a bunch of other trace elements. But of course that wouldn't create a person; it would only create a swamp—because the sum of the parts doesn't achieve the whole. It takes a little biochemical magic as well.

Productive Team Dynamics

Assembling the team. Nearly every IEP (Individualized Education Program) or other form of school team I've ever seen, my own and others, succeeded or struggled based on the team leader or lack of a definitive leader. A productive team will have at its nucleus a "proton," a leader with a positive charge who sets the tone, establishes and maintains the underlying current that guides the team interactions, and sets up the formulas and processes that offer the best chances for progress. Defining who's on the team or who needs to be added to or dropped from the team (not a good fit for the child, or services no longer needed) has to be the first step. In many cases, team members may be dictated by the IEP or other formal document. But if that isn't the case, a strong core starting team for most autistic children would consist of the parent(s) or caregiver(s), the classroom teacher, the special educator, and, because few autistic children are without sensory and social communication issues, an occupational therapist and a speech/language pathologist. It can grow from there, and the composition of the team will change and evolve as the child does.

Communication, communication, communication. Just as location, location, location is everything in real estate, communication is everything in teamwork.

- Between home and school.

  - Daily: There's no overstating the value of communication between home and school, on a daily basis if possible. It's a long time between 3:00 PM and 8:00 AM, let alone weekends, holidays, snow days, and other breaks in routine. Much can happen in those hours that will impact the student's school day. It's a long time between 8:00 AM and 3:00 PM for a parent or caregiver, too. What does the child do all day? When they come home, they're exhausted and don't want to or aren't able to converse. Regular communication between home and school enhances team members' ability to support each other's efforts and adds a consistency to the child's routine that smooths out the daily transitions. It can head off some problems, nip others in the bud, and celebrate achievements in both settings. It communicates to the child that we're all on the same team.

    Daily communication needn't be prohibitively time-consuming. It can be as simple as a bullet-pointed text or email, with or without added commentary. A spiral notebook that goes back and forth with the student each day can be a workable option for families without easy access to technology. The important thing is to recognize it as the ounce of effort that saves pounds of guessing, defensive reacting, or simply not knowing.

  - Overall: Parents, a teacher pal of mine asked me to be sure to tell you: "Don't assume I know everything about your child. I may only have the prior year's academic information and perhaps no personal information at all. Be a resource for us, a bridge between programs."

    Teachers, you know that many non-autistic kids give their parents little information about their school day. For your students with autism, this is magnified by their difficulty with verbalization, sequencing, generalization, and retrieval, not to mention the exhaustion they feel after an entire day's effort of having to "hold it together," battling sensory and social challenges and a ceaseless stream of expectations they may or may not understand and may or may not be able to meet. Don't make their parents or caregivers beg you for information.

- Between members of the team within a school: Productive team members recognize that shared information and exchange of ideas is what makes the necessary division of labor work. It also communicates on a wider platform those same shared discoveries and concerns between home and school.

Recognizing the entire class as a team or community, working as a whole, toward inclusion. "This is how society works successfully," asserts elementary school teacher Roneete Lynas, who describes herself as "a huge advocate and proponent of the 'classroom community.' There should be no reason why students and teachers alike are not sharing the responsibility of including *all* learners." Knowing how to work as a member of a community is as crucial a life skill as anything coming out of a book.

Promoting a cycle of encouragement and reward—not only teacher to student, but student to student and teacher to teacher. Instilling the idea of taking responsibility for one's self should be the first step, not the end goal. "Life rewards us for acting responsibly," Lynas adds, "but we benefit more fully and more wholly when acting cooperatively." The class team who together reaps either reward or consequence learns a lesson that they'll carry into the workplace, interpersonal relationships, and civic life in general as adults: that they have the power to create the most successful environment if working as a team.

Giving each other the courtesy of a clean slate. Parents may have had bad experiences with previous teachers or schools, but projecting past conflicts or issues onto a new teacher, "coming in with guns blazing before you even have a chance to get to know me or my program," as one put it, is counterproductive. *This is what's happened in the past and I expect the same from you* sets up a dangerous scenario for both teachers and parents. Teachers, your previous experiences with ASD students and their parents/caregivers, whether frustrating or successful, may have little relevance to your current student.

> **Life rewards us for acting responsibly, but we benefit more fully and wholly when acting cooperatively.**

An understanding that the team is not static. The team should and must evolve as the child grows and changes. Listen as objectively as possible when one team member says something isn't working. When transition to a new setting, team member, or approach seems necessary, let it happen in the spirit of wanting a common good for the child. Evaluate as neutrally as possible: if the child is struggling too hard in the current placement or situation, it's time to find a better environment.

Eyes on the goal. The team recognizes that the job of parents/caregivers and educators is to prepare this young person for meaningful adult life wherein his success will depend upon much more than test scores and transcripts. Even in the face of today's crushing test requirements, Roneete Lynas prompts us to "remind ourselves that students aren't under our instruction to become little experts, merely regurgitating information. Rather, they're placed in our hands to be guided through the year. They're truly practicing for real life, for the entire course of this school year—until the next comes, with its new expectations."

Indifferent Team Dynamics

"It's not my job." An attitude that the so-called special needs student is someone else's responsibility is the hallmark of indifferent team dynamics. It's the classroom teacher who says, "I have thirty other students. He's the responsibility of the resource teacher (or the paraeducator)." It's the parent who says, "I feed and clothe him. You're the school—so teach him."

Good teams can fall apart quickly when members rely, either consciously or out of benign neglect, on someone else to do the heavy lifting. An effective team stays strong when all members contribute applicable and timely information regarding both the individual child and the state of current knowledge, research, and attitudes about the disability itself. This sharing of responsibility and insight is the only sensible way for everyone to keep up as needed in a field like autism, where knowledge, understanding, identification, and integration are on a swift and steep ascent.

Accepting "good enough" as good enough. It's the principal who says, "He talks, doesn't he? Why does he need speech therapy?" It's the team who says, "We understand ASDs, and our students make progress. We don't need more training." It's the teacher or parent who assumes that if the child isn't disruptive in class, there must not be any issues, so why take the time and effort to do a sensory profile? Or the playground monitor who watches a student with autism keep to himself at recess, thinking he must be choosing to not join his peers, so there's no need for social facilitation.

Just because the wheel doesn't squeak doesn't mean it's revolving smoothly. Knowing a child has autism should be enough to spark our curiosity about behaviors and reactions that aren't typical, even when—especially when—those behaviors and reactions aren't disruptive. Too often, this is the child who slips through the cracks, her disability seemingly invisible as the clues in plain sight are misunderstood or overlooked, never receiving the sensory and social communication services that will be so critical to her overall success and to which she's entitled.

Complacency is a malaise. New information, new thought about teaching students with ASDs, comes in a constant stream, with much invaluable insight now coming from autistic adults describing their experiences as students. It's there and at the ready for teams wanting to work better, smarter, and more effectively with the autistic child.

Choosing reactive over proactive. Responding to problems only as they arise rather than anticipating and preventing them ultimately diminishes results for both you and your student and is a truly inefficient use of your teaching time and her learning time. Consider the difference between *survive* and *thrive*. Yes, it's sometimes all we can do to survive the moment or the situation. I've been known to respond to the platitude "Never give up!" with "Let go or be dragged." It happens. But most of us want to look back on our careers as professionals or parents as embodied by striving to see the child in our charge thrive.

Allowing anything less than a zero-tolerance policy on bullying and teasing. Good team dynamics demand that all team members guide each other toward appropriate behaviors by modeling healthy interactions. "'Typical' students often, if allowed to, reject the child who socializes or interacts differently," says Roneete Lynas. "It's critical that the teacher validate to the whole class each attempt the student with autism makes at socializing in his or her own way, placing the emphasis on what the student can do rather than what he cannot do. It introduces the reality to the class as a whole that all people do not act similarly and that it's important to accept differences."

"This is the way we always do it." *Always* and *never* are absolutes. It only takes one exception to negate an always or a never, and that exception is often the child with autism. Even the respected fallback of "best practices" has to be examined in the light of each unique autistic child. Best practices are only average practices if doggedly applied to every student; anything that today is a best practice (or "evidence-based") began with someone's observation of something non-standard. "Best practices" are not best if executed poorly (not factoring in details such as in what environment, for how long, who administers the practices, and how outcomes are evaluated) or if everyone's doing them and not paying attention to the children who fall outside of them.

The spectrum nature of autism automatically negates the idea that there can be a one-size-fits-all program or mentality for teaching students with ASDs. Yes—teaching students with ASDs can be a measure more challenging than teaching typically developing non-autistic students. Commensurate results hang in the balance. When your student is young, it may seem like there's all the time in the world to work toward those results, and in fact there may be several thousand days filled with learning opportunity remaining in her school years, but from a parent's standpoint, moments of truth arrive all too soon.

This Tale of Two Teachers occurred in my older son Connor's last years of high school. A student with ADHD, he never failed to produce above-average work in homework, projects, and class discussions. Tests were another story, the results frequently failing to accurately capture how much he knew. Working with an outside education specialist during his freshman year, we were able to document how his brain stored and retrieved information differently than what a typical school test demanded. Because Connor didn't meet the bar for an IEP, the school counselor advised us to work out alternatives with each individual teacher. And therein we discovered how vast can be the range of effort and attitude among teachers and their willingness to accommodate a nonstandard learner. One agreed to weight the homework more heavily than the tests. One offered extra credit projects to bridge the gap. One agreed to test orally. Some were unresponsive. Two were flat-out belligerent. In the end, it came down to a microcosm of two teachers. I met with the first to explore what testing accommodations she could make for his learning differences. The response was "None. If he wants to go to college, he has to learn to take a test." He eked a C out of the class, and that was the end of his career in that subject.

The second teacher, in only her fourth year of teaching, met my request for testing accommodation with gusto. "Whatever he needs is what we're going to do," she said. "I see no reason why he won't be successful in my class. And we're going to have a lot of fun too." And that's exactly what happened. He soared, chose to continue the subject in college, and was later able to make use of it in the workplace.

Indifference will make a difference. But not the kind any of us wants.

Poisonous Team Dynamics

Combat mentality: the number-one deterrent to successful team building. Teacher or parent, a combative attitude impedes our ability to make progress with an autistic student. "Our relationship must be an alliance, not an adversarial face-off," says a middle school special educator. "We're all working in the same direction. Our common interest is the child. It should never be about me vs. you or whether we like each other."

The Blame Game: undermining each other undermines the student's learning. Here's the fascinating point-counterpoint. Teachers want parents to know: communicating to your child that everything that's going wrong is the school's fault undermines your child's ability to trust me, to comply with necessary classroom boundaries, and, ultimately, to learn. Parents want teachers to know: the behavior you're describing is utterly inconsistent with what I see at home and therefore hard to believe. How do I know that this behavior isn't my child's reaction to someone's unkindness or incompetence?

Oh, what a delicate line.

Never should we put the child in the middle of this tug-of-war. Whatever the situation, it can't always be one party's fault any more than it can always be someone else's fault. Teacher and parent must both step back and hear each other as objectively as possible when faced with information that makes their emotional level rise. Understand how common it is for children to exhibit a different set of behaviors at school than they do at home, and vice versa. And while your first reaction may naturally and understandably be defensive, know that most times, you don't need to offer an immediate response. It's okay to say, "This is new information for me. I need to think about it and get back to you."

Failing to distinguish between assertive and aggressive. The difference between being assertive and being aggressive is often the element of anger—and anger always has a cost: it costs us in trust, and it costs us in potentially vital information.

Teachers appreciate the parent who's a knowledgeable, effective advocate for their child, firm but respectful. That's far removed from being a fist-pounder. Says one elementary school resource teacher: "In an ideal world, I want to share with the parent any inside perspective or off-the-record knowledge I have about the system and how they might navigate it to the benefit of their child. But if I sense in any way that the parent will use the information in a way that comes back on me or threatens my job, it's only natural that I will not share."

This cuts both ways. Parents have told me: "I see teachers stubbornly clinging to methods that they claim have worked with other kids, methods that I know from experience don't work with my child. I could save them a lot of wasted time and effort, but if I sense in any way that the school will use my information to try to cut future services, I have no choice but to remain silent. Meanwhile, my child doesn't progress at the rate he might otherwise."

A sixth-grade teacher agrees, lamenting the cost in lost learning time: "Time spent on procedural concerns translates into less time actually teaching. Combative parents mean I have to spend additional time anticipating confrontations, documenting my work beyond what's usual—covering my back, really—rather than engaging in activities that directly benefit the student: teaching, preparing, researching, lesson planning, professional reading."

This too cuts both ways. "I dare not think about the hours I spend on phone calls, letters and meetings, trying to get our defiant school to comply with the requirements of the IEP," says one mom. "That's time I could be spending reading with my child, helping with homework, drawing, playing, or talking with her—any of which would be more beneficial to all of us."

Beneficial to all of us. That captures it, wouldn't you say? Great teams don't just happen; they're thoughtfully constructed. I like to think of it as a tapestry in which we, the lifelong learners and teachers, are the threads. Look at the back of any tapestry and you'll see numerous colors, hundreds of threads of all lengths, many of their beginnings buried under other threads and their ends hanging, cut to size. All of us are in it together, parents and caregivers paddling through eddies of programs, treatments, and instructors. Teachers tossed in a sea of children who come and go with the annual tide. And the child himself—the one to whom it's actually happening, riding the whitewater of not only autism, not only of other medical or economic conditions, but of many typical aspects of child development as well.

Yes, the back of that tapestry looks like an unruly mess. But turn it over to the front, and the chaos vanishes. It's a thing of beauty, each stitch individual yet absolutely necessary to the whole. Far more than the sum of its threads, Team Tapestry crafts a work of art.

Chapter Three

I Think Differently

Teach me in a way that's meaningful to me

My millennial children don't know whether to be amused or aghast at how their parents grew up in an era without disks, cell phones, computers, streaming, and instant communication. Back in the frontier days when I got my first computer, you either had an Apple MacIntosh or an IBM personal computer. The Macs and the PCs were the tech version of the infamous feuding families, the Hatfields and McCoys. Macs and PCs not only didn't talk to each other, they couldn't talk to each other. They didn't "think" alike.

Your autistic student is like those early Macs in a PC-dominated environment. He's hard-wired differently. Not incorrectly, not weirdly, not unnaturally—just differently.

Macs and PCs couldn't communicate with each other because their operating systems weren't compatible. Everything about the Mac's architecture and command structure was unlike the PC's. If you've been a lifelong user of a particular operating system, you may consider yourself fairly computer-competent and may not be aware of how foreign it feels trying to navigate an unfamiliar system. I found out. During Bryce's third grade year with Jackie, I volunteered for a year-long project that involved transferring some of the kids' writings to computer files. I figured on doing it at home in my off-work hours. Then I was told the work couldn't be done on my PC at home; it had to be done on Macs, in the classroom.

I'll spare you the details of the learning curve I never conquered. Week after week, I thought I'd learned enough about the Mac operating system to do the project, only to run into new language or command obstacles. The project I'd thought would be enjoyable became a jaw-clenching exercise in anxiety. Why? Because fifteen years of day-in and day-out banging away on a PC had entrenched the Windows operating system so deeply in my brain that I was completely blindsided by how hard it was to put it aside, even temporarily, and learn to interact with a system that "thought" differently. My own processing speed slowed to a crawl.

Welcome to life as a student with autism, whose brain architecture and basic operating system are unlike those of most people not on the autism spectrum. Macs and PCs made their debuts in the 1980s. Their compatibility issues weren't resolved until the early 2000s. Your student doesn't have twenty years, and luckily, along the way, the Macs and the PCs have evolved to where their differences aren't as great as they once were. However, the question here is: have we become more flexible in our own thinking to appreciate the value that both types of brains bring?

Learning to relate to the different ways the autism brain processes the world around it can be challenging because we have to be willing to step outside so-called "normalcy." Nowhere is this divide wider than in the area of social processing and social communication.

Collectively we're a social-driven society, the majority of us learning about and processing social and environmental inputs in a similar manner. Across all currents of life, our non-autistic thinking patterns are naturally shared and naturally reinforced. Adults assume kids will learn to "be social" through "normal" development. We expect this social know-how to bud, blossom, and grow in our children, generally without us pairing it with much concrete teaching. To be able to understand a fundamentally dissimilar way of brain processing requires you to suspend all you know and go somewhere you didn't even know existed. That takes courage. But that's where we must go if our goal as teachers is to be effective with our autistic students.

To be able to understand a fundamentally dissimilar way of brain processing requires you to suspend all you know and go somewhere you didn't even know existed. That takes courage.

This endeavor begins with a critical distinction: this differently wired brain has nothing to do with your student's desire to learn. Some students will have brains whose hard-wiring makes them capable of physically developing the environment for perspective-taking, while others will not. Within their individual parameters, most can improve, and we will never know the full extent of a student's abilities unless we establish communication via the architecture he has in place. The Apple Mac in Bryce's third grade classroom wasn't incompetent or "challenged." The computer didn't fail; I failed. I failed to comprehend its operating system, failed to input data in a format it could process. We must disabuse ourselves forever of the idea that our student with autism "could do it if he only tried harder." Child psychologist Ross W. Green, PhD, author of *The Explosive Child* and *Lost at School*, advances the widely embraced idea that "kids do well if they can," meaning that when they have the skills to process what's happening around them and respond in a socially expected manner and communicate adaptively, they do. Absent being taught those skills, they can't.

Also throw away the idea that all you have to do is "try harder." If we aren't trying through compatible channels, we can try until we cry and it will only be a demonstration of the proverbial definition of insanity: doing the same thing over and over yet expecting a different result. We have to try smarter and more empathetically and try through an alternate lens, through the child's own learning modality.

This difference in architecture impacts critical thinking (classification, comparison, application), executive management (attention, planning, and memory functions) and social pragmatics (perspective-taking). These abilities are missing from many autistic students' hard-wiring. But with compassionate and consistent instruction and coaching, many children with ASDs can and do expand their social competence, improve executive functioning, and achieve a functional degree of flexibility in thinking and conversing (relative to their own starting point, not that of peers or siblings). The goal is that the child will be able to observe and gauge the world around her in a problem-solving way, to understand the "why" behind our social behaviors, and to be able to interact in a manner that enables her to reach her social goals.

Books such as Dr. Temple Grandin and Sean Barron's *Unwritten Rules of Social Relationships* or the anecdotal insights of author Jennifer McIlwee Myers recounted later in this book offer up raw, eye-opening accounts of how children with autism spectrum disorders must navigate the non-autistic world. For some, the approach will be logical in the extreme, perhaps even to the point of appearing cold. For others, their journey will be fraught with emotional turbulence as they valiantly attempt to fit into society while inherently lacking the essential understanding of how to do so. No two children with ASD are alike, but all their stories echo a common denominator: individual teachers had the power to make or break their will to stay the course and achieve.

How Thinking and Processing Is Different in Autism

Every day offers numerous opportunities to help our autistic students understand society's patterns of communicating and relating, and to teach the skills for functional communication and relating that can be so foreign to the autism brain. Keep in mind always the spectrum nature of autism. While the traits described here may be characteristic, they'll vary widely in degree from mild to profound.

The One—and Only?—Learning Channel

Students with autism often have one-channel wiring in a polyphonic world. They likely process most information via the one learning intelligence that works best for them. In most students with autism, this will be visual or tactile, or less commonly, auditory. They struggle to process multiple simultaneously occurring sensory modalities. For instance, they can listen, engage in movement activities, or talk, but they may falter when required to process more than one of these tasks at a time. It can be especially difficult to listen and write at the same time (take notes in class), or even to converse and make eye contact at the same time, a common demand which many autistic adults describe as physically painful, nausea- or shock-inducing, paralyzing, or just plain creepy ("like being forced to lick the end of a battery," according to a participant in a 2017 National Institutes of Health study). The seamless integration among the senses that happens within the non-autistic brain is often missing in your student's brain.

Equally difficult is shifting back and forth between modalities (such as from visual to auditory and back again), and filtering out irrelevant sensory distractions: being able to distinguish the teacher's voice over the buzz of the flies on the window sill, the garbage truck rolling by the window outside, and the band practice down the hall. One-channel processing coupled with the inability to filter can contribute to the autistic student's hyper-focused and repetitive behaviors. Constantly under a barrage of sensory chaos, they become physically and emotionally exhausted. Those single-focus or repetitive behaviors you may observe are a self-regulation technique that calms and soothes them. It's the only way they know to respond to defend themselves.

A Zillion Parts in Search of a Whole

The non-autistic brain thinks general-to-specific. Your students with autism think specific-to-general. Consider how acute that difference is. For them, each bit of information taken in exists in separate, discrete boxes in their brain. For us, bits of data naturally, effort-lessly sift into categories and subcategories and sub-subcategories. Did you have to consciously learn that bananas, apples, grapes, and watermelons make up the category called fruit? Bet you didn't; the category "fruit" just made sense.

Our brain organizes the information we take in and even cross-references it for us. Not so for your autistic student. Categorical thinking is difficult for them and must be taught. Their brain is like a cavernous warehouse filled with bits of unrelated information. As their teacher, you need to help them learn to organize, label, and associate all that information. It begins with teaching the child to think in categories.

In the young child, the categories may be few and unrelated. This is partly why your student will often respond with answers that relate only vaguely to the question. He has only a limited number of categories in which to slot the new information, and in his mind, it has to fit into one of them. His organizational ability will develop and expand over time if, as more information is taken in, we teach him how to put it into categories with increasing complexity as he learns to compare and contrast things tangible and intangible (such as motivations and intentions—again, the "why" of social behavior). Those categories then become subcategories of other larger categories, and so on.

As you let this characteristic of the autism architecture sink in, you may—and should—find it overwhelming to conceive of every piece of information in your head existing independently of any other thought. What would it be like to have no ability to organize information and create associations? It's no wonder your student has difficulty learning. Wouldn't you?

Your student's trouble with categorizing often has an equally formidable cousin: an impaired ability to generalize information. As we've discussed, for the child with autism, every new experience may exist in a vacuum. There's no "whole," no umbrella under which different-but-related ideas or experiences can gather. They don't generalize a new experience to prior experiences or knowledge until they're taught to do so. If you teach them to safely cross the street at the intersection of Main and Smith Streets, that learning doesn't automatically apply to the situation that has them standing at the intersection of 23rd Avenue and Johnson Drive. To their way of thinking, it's not the same.

Teach them: to *categorize*. Start with concrete categories like colors, clothes, or vehicles, and build to categories that are less concrete, like function and proximity, or social categories like feelings and facial expressions. Explain why an object fits into one category or several but not in others. Have them *compare and contrast* similarities and differences.

Teach them: to *apply concepts*. Help them understand that categories can represent concepts, that information can be inter-related, and that you can take what you know about particular situations and people and objects and use it in other settings and situations.

Teach them: to *identify cause and effect*. Like information, the actions and reactions of people and objects don't exist discretely either. Relationships can be affected by choice. Start with concrete examples and work up from there. If you leave your Hot Wheels out in the rain, they'll rust. If you bop Alex, he won't want to play with you. If you ignore Erica, her feelings will be hurt. Actions elicit reactions, and many of the consequences of our actions are within our power to control and affect. Teach your student: isn't having that control great?

I Need to See It to Learn It

Many of your autistic students will be visual/spatial learners—they think in pictures rather than words. They might tell you:

I need to see something to learn it, not just hear it. Words are frequently like steam to me—I know they're there, but they evaporate before I have a chance to make sense of them. I need more time to deal with infor-mation than most of my classmates. Instructions or directions delivered in words come and go in an instant, and I don't have instant-processing skills. When information is presented to me visually, it can stay in front of me for as long as it takes for me to think it through and understand it. Otherwise, I live the constant frustration of knowing that I'm missing big blocks of what you're trying to teach, can't do what you're expecting of me, and am helpless to do anything about it.

Whole Chunk Learning

Your student on the spectrum may be a *gestalt* learner, absorbing information in chunks, rather than the more widely accepted, analytical step-by-step learning process. He watches and watches from the sidelines as other children pick up and perform skills and tasks he can't do. Then one day, he up and does it. His language development may begin the same way, with echolalia (memorized scripts or whole blocks of language) rather than one-word-at-a-time learning.

Processing information in whole pieces like this compromises the child's ability to assign inferential meaning to the parts of the whole. He may be able to sing the "Star-Spangled Banner" or "O Canada" but have no concept of what a national anthem is. Unfortunately, most academic curriculum is built upon an analytic learning structure— the antithesis of optimal instruction to the child with autism who learns in a gestalt manner. Though not adequately recognized, gestalt learning is not a lesser way to learn. It is valid, it is acceptable, it is another legitimate way to learn.

Over and Over and Over Again

The behaviors of autistic children are frequently characterized by excessive selectivity and hyper-focus (rigidity and repetition). Their extreme dependence on routine and sameness is a result of a brain architecture that has difficulty processing change. Even small variations from expectation, such as taking a detour route to school, having a substitute teacher, or changing the students' desks around may create cognitive chaos that can domino-affect the entire course of the day.

Our student might explain it this way:

You may view my behavior and thinking as rigid, but sameness and routine are my life-lines to being able to handle the details of daily life that you take for granted. Knowing that parts of my day and my life will be the same every time helps me cope with the constant anxiety of living in a baffling world that seems to be in constant and unpredictable motion. I do want to learn to interact with you and my surroundings. So please respect my fears and ease me out of my inflexibility gently, until I learn the skills that will make me more able to tolerate my environment and until you understand how to adapt my environment so that I can learn. Within the safety of my comfort zone, give me practical, concrete, hands-on experiences that help me see and live the benefits of flexibility. Help me move out of my rigidity one baby step at a time.

Teach her: to think *flexibly* and *cohesively*. With thoughtful planning on our part that includes frequent, incremental opportunities for practice, she can learn to take life's little speed bumps without bottoming out. Where she's excessively selective and hyper-focused, teach—through your words and actions—that

- there is more than one way to view a situation

- problems can have more than one solution

- ideas can be expressed and exchanged in many ways

- there is more than one "right" way to do most things

- there is meaning in communication beyond what we see and hear

Teach your student the power of having a Plan B or C or D, that problem-solving is easier when we remember to ask "I wonder"

54

questions (more about that in Chapter Seven), and that knowing when to ask for help is equally as important as getting the answer right. Teach her to expect unpredictability as part of life and social interaction, and that it not only is necessary but can even at times lead to fun and unanticipated enjoyment.

A One-Sided Coin

Many autistic students think in concrete terms, meaning they will interpret what you say in a very literal manner. Tell him to "shake a leg" and don't be surprised if he does just that. He's not being impudent—he's following your instruction. Real-life examples abound. One mom told me how she asked her autistic daughter in the back seat of the car to "crack a window." The girl replied, "Really? Well, okay," and hurled her backpack at the window. Metaphors, idioms, and figurative language aren't part of an autistic child's mindset unless specifically taught.

In the classroom, this can result in difficulty with exercises that ask the student to summarize or synthesize, or pick out the theme or main point. It affects the manner in which he's able to retrieve information. He might respond well to prompted retrieval, such as a multiple-choice or matching quiz. Difficulty skyrockets when he's faced with tasks entailing open-ended recall without aid of prompting or cueing. A vivid example of this came when Bryce scored low on a social studies test requiring him to fill in a map of the United States with each state's name. We'd studied for this test together, so I knew that the low score didn't even come close to reflecting his actual knowledge. The teacher agreed to retest by giving him a map with the first letter of each state, saying, "I want to know how much he knows, in whatever way he needs to communicate it to me." With those minimal prompts (which wouldn't have helped him if he truly didn't know the material), Bryce aced the test.

On the more advanced level, your student's concrete thinking means that abstract concepts and groupings may be quite difficult for him. He might be able to come up with categories such as zoo animals, types of trucks, or foods that are vegetables—concrete subjects. But he may struggle with abstract categories such as things that spin, things that make you sneeze, things that live in water. Or, even more nebulous: things that make you happy, things that are opposites, things that are luxuries.

Everyone Thinks Like Me—Don't They?

Perspective-taking abilities, called theory of mind (ToM) skills, may be significantly impaired in your autistic student. Until they're taught ToM skills, they may assume that everyone everywhere shares their way of thinking, their thoughts about a person, event, or situation, and their points of view. That difficulty generalizing applies here, too. So, explaining someone's point of view in one instance doesn't mean your student understands that all people can have different ways of thinking in every different instance.

Perspective-taking is a social skill that involves knowing and understanding that the same words, events, or objects may look, sound, or feel different to individual people. It's considering the thoughts, feelings, attitudes, and beliefs of others before we speak or act. Many of the social-emotional gaps in your autistic student stem from this lesser perspective-taking ability. She can't anticipate what others might say or do in various situations, nor understand that what one person does in a given situation, another person may never do. Your student may not even understand that other people have thoughts and emotions, and thus she may behave in ways that come across as uncaring or self-centered.

Michelle Garcia Winner, a speech-language pathologist widely known for teaching "social thinking" to individuals with ASDs, is the author of two monumental books that address many of these social brains processing differences, *Thinking About YOU Thinking About ME* and *Think Social! A Social Thinking® Curriculum for School-Aged Students*. Both are invaluable reading for all teachers and parents. In her books, Winner defines the critical elements of perspective-taking as the ability to *actively consider* and *adjust to*:

- The thoughts and emotions of others as well as oneself, even if no direct interaction is taking place

- Similarities and differences in religious, political, and cultural beliefs between your own and those of others

- Using prior knowledge and experiences as they pertain to communicating with others

- The motives and intentions of one's self and others, even if there is no direct interaction

Without being taught these perspective-taking skills, your autistic student may never experience the results and rewards of healthy social thinking and processing detailed by Winner:

- To interpret the needs and wants of others

- To provide responses that are considered empathetic

- To safely navigate around persons who may have ill intentions

- To interact with nuance so that others don't perceive them to be too demanding or too straightforward

- To share in the passions or delights of others even without sharing the same level of interest in the topic purely because one can enjoy the underlying relationship that's evolving

- To engage in acts of socially related critical thinking and personal problem solving

Perspective-taking isn't a standalone thing you teach your student. It's an extremely wide and interrelated pool of social, emotional, and conceptual processing that works synergistically. This is an area that you will teach only as much as the child's brain will understand at a time (because the pace of learning to take perspective is deeply personal), and generally this teaching and learning spans years, not terms or semesters. That said, being able to think

Hold top-of-mind that perspective-taking ability is unrelated to intelligence: IQ or language capabilities aren't indicators of perspective-taking abilities.

about and interpret one's own thoughts, feelings, and behaviors and those of others is the core of social functioning and of understanding the social world and all its happenings.

Teach your student: that people have different ways of thinking, feeling, and responding. That we not only respond to others but initiate contact with others. That we share and reciprocate actions with others, not merely attempt to control our own situation. That we take social cues from others without imitating their exact behaviors and words. That we engage in cooperative and reciprocal give- and-take, not just parallel activity with others. Do all this, and more, in concrete, meaningful ways to the child's learning style. Make it real—to them. Simply discussing these concepts, providing real-world examples, pointing out when others are trying to imagine the thoughts and feelings of a partner, a classmate, won't be enough. If it were, the child would already be able to take perspective.

And it's important to hold top-of-mind that perspective-taking ability is unrelated to intelligence: having a high IQ or advanced language capabilities (or lack thereof) isn't an indicator of perspective-taking abilities. Bryce's high school principal emphasized repeatedly that lack of social competence "will get you fired from a job faster than lack of cognitive skills or intelligence." Perspective-taking ability, part of that social competence, is widely considered an essential skill for success in the workplace, an aspiration most parents hold for their autistic children.

Start to See Things Differently

Remember the old cliché that everyone learns to put their pants on one leg at a time? Bryce didn't. When he was learning to dress himself, he found it more expedient to sit on the edge of the bed, roll back, throw his legs up in the air and put his pants on both legs at the same time, all in one movement. He visualized it in a way that made more sense to him, applied a motor-planning sequence that made more sense to him, and came up with his own, efficient approach to a common life skill. The fact that 99 percent of the world puts their pants on one leg at a time doesn't make his way wrong, and for some, his way might be better.

Teaching our autistic children will be an exercise in spitting into the wind if we're not willing to accept and respect that their brains process information differently, and then find effective ways to adapt our teaching accordingly. If we can't manage to be flexible in our approach to teaching him, if we don't accept his whole self—mental, physical, metaphysical, emotional, cognitive—as valid and worthy of our effort, we can't expect him to respond with any degree of motivation or desire to connect to us or our social environment.

The sweet spot is a meeting place somewhere in the middle. We shift our thinking enough to teach to his way of thinking and processing in a meaningful way. Then he can learn to be more comfortable with our way of thinking and to feel competent in a non-autistic world. Little by little the familiarity between us grows. Macs now communicate with PCs, and the 21st century brought about the first annual Hatfields and McCoys Reunion Festival. There's never been a better time to learn to inhabit that diverse perspective. You and your student will both learn things you never knew you never knew.

Chapter Four

Behavior Is Communication: Yours, Mine, and Ours

Behavior is probably the most discussed, debated, dreaded, and often misunderstood issue within autism. It's the concern that's launched a thousand parent-teacher meetings, yet again as many medical and therapy consultations and miles-long social media threads. It's the fire-breathing dragon, the Goliath, the T-Rex, and the Titanic hitting the iceberg—sometimes all at once.

And yet behavior is a greatly weakened enemy once we accept a basic truth: that behavior never, ever "comes out of nowhere." There's always an underlying trigger, an unmet need. Once we identify the trigger, we're three-quarters of the way to disabling it. Yes, it requires that we invest time and effort in sleuth work. You may have heard the term "behavior detective" or "social detective" discussed in education venues. Before you start wilting at the thought of how time-intensive this approach might be, consider that the upfront investment of effort spent on behavior prevention pales to nothing against the draining, unproductive alternative of having to react over and over to the same *preventable* behavior.

There are tools that make this job far less daunting than it seems. We'll head to the tool shed in a minute. But first, a couple of prerequisites for using these tools:

> **Stop thinking in terminology such as bad behavior, misbehavior, negative behavior. Behavior is behavior, period.**

1. Stop thinking in terminology such as bad behavior, misbehavior, negative behavior. Behavior is behavior, period. Some behaviors may be situationally inappropriate or unexpected, but a great deal of what autistic children do springs from misunderstanding, misinterpreting, or simply not observing their social surrounds. Fully accept and embrace as fact that all behavior is a form of communication, often the only mode for one who has been taught no other functional form. Remember always that teaching isn't teaching if they didn't learn it, and that teaching rules or skills without the social-emotional connectivity needed to put it in meaningful, relevant context isn't teaching much at all.

2. In trying to pinpoint underlying reasons for a child's behavior, we must first look at our own. We have to acknowledge that our own behavior is information we impart to the child about his environment. We can't question what his behavior is telling us without also questioning what our behavior is telling him.

I also urge you to be as gentle in your efforts to change a child's behavior as you could reasonably expect of yourself. It strikes me as sheer lunacy how much we expect of our students with ASDs in the area of behavior modification when we as adults find it so difficult to accomplish ourselves. Every darn New Year's, out come the same tired old behavior-modification resolutions: lose weight, eat healthier, stop smoking, spend less money, exercise more, get organized. By the end of January, it's usually all over but the shouting. What right do we have to expect greater inner fortitude of a child living with perpetual neurological challenge than we're able to muster ourselves?

The thing is, we frequently set ourselves up for failure because taking on three or four New Year's resolutions is too many, too much. We all know too well how demoralizing it is to accept that we didn't keep any of those resolutions, didn't manage to change our behavior. How much better it would be to pick one achievable goal at a time, to experience incremental success and the feeling of self-worth that comes with it before moving on to the next challenge. And so it is, if not more so, for a child.

We can't hit on the answers to all behavior issues in one chapter of one small book, and we won't try. There are dozens of excellent books devoted solely to behavior; you may have already read some of them. But this book focuses

> **We can't question what a child's behavior is telling us without first questioning what our behavior is telling him.**

not only on the child's behavior, but in equal part on our adult behavior and the role it plays in the equation. Let's take a big-picture look at some factors that can influence behavior in the educational setting. Who better to explain his own behavior, and tell us how he perceives ours, than our child himself?

Our autistic student says:

- Look for sensory issues first. Many of my behaviors come from sensory discomfort. The classroom is too bright or too loud or there's too much on the walls to distract me. Maybe I need to sit closer to you—I don't understand what you're saying because there are too many noises in between, like that lawnmower outside the window, Jasmine whispering to Tanya, chairs scraping, pencil sharpener grinding. And sitting in a chair may not be my best learning position. My sense of equilibrium isn't like yours, and I sometimes can't tell where the edge of the seat is—am I about to fall off? Maybe I could do my reading lying on a mat (full-length body contact is calming for me) or a beanbag chair, or using one of those adjustable standing desks?

Ask my occupational therapist for sensory-friendly ideas for the classroom. It's actually good for all kids, not just me.

- Allow me self-regulation breaks before I need them. A quiet, carpeted corner of the room with some pillows, books, and headphones allows me a place to go to re-group when I feel overwhelmed but is still close enough that I can rejoin the classroom activity smoothly. Or maybe I need some movement—an errand to the office or a lap around the gym with a peer buddy may be all it takes.

- Keep a behavior detective notes about when and where I'm having trouble. What activity are we doing, what time is it, and who's around me? Try to become aware of the many sensory and social things about our surroundings. See. Hear. Feel. Smell. The things you may easily tune out may be the very things that are causing me discomfort, even pain. You're going to be amazed at how much this may reveal about why I react and behave the way I do.

- Don't make a bad situation worse. I don't want to or choose to melt down, show anger, or otherwise disrupt our classroom. You can help me get over it more quickly by not responding with unkind or angry behavior of your own. The way you respond to me can prolong rather than end a bad episode:

- Raising the pitch or volume of your voice. I hear the shouting, but not the words.

- Mocking or mimicking me. I often don't recognize sarcasm, and insults or name-calling won't embarrass me out of my behavior. What it does teach me is that I can't trust you to guide me respectfully.

- Making accusations you can't back up. If you don't have solid proof that I did it, you're just guessing. What if you're wrong?

- Using a double standard. Making me follow rules or expectations that the rest of the class doesn't not only makes it harder for me socially, but also squashes my self-esteem and affects my classmates' willingness to work with me as a peer.

- Comparing me or my efforts to those of a sibling or other student.

- Bringing up previous or unrelated things that have happened.

- Lumping me into a general category by saying things like "kids like you all do this."

If you do fall into one of these, you can still make things better with a sincere apology. I'm trying to learn that everyone gets angry or frustrated and messes up sometimes, even you, and that even when the mistake looks huge, we can still put it right and move on.

- If you're not getting through, try another way. My mom says it's the definition of insanity to keep doing things the same way and expect a different result. If you keep doing or saying the same things but my behavior isn't changing, maybe the behavior that needs to change is yours. You have no idea how bad it feels to know that adults think my behavior is willful, that I could change my reactions to my environment if I wanted to badly enough. It isn't, and I can't. You haven't found the root cause of my behavior yet; please keep looking! When your teaching isn't working, I'm sitting here hoping you'll change the teaching.

Jennifer McIlwee Myers, author of *How to Teach Life Skills to Kids with Autism or Asperger's* and *Growing Up with Sensory Issues: Insider Tips from a Woman with Autism*, recalls a childhood with Asperger's syndrome and now, as an adult, still experiences its challenges. She has painful memories of a teacher who chose a mean-spirited approach to her behavior, thereby missing enormous learning opportunities for a student who learned eagerly but differently. Jennifer tells this unvarnished story:

> In third grade, I got in trouble during almost every vocabulary lesson. The routine was: we looked up the words in our dictionaries and wrote the definitions. Then Mrs. Attitude (name changed to protect the guilty) went over the words with the class. The problem for me was, I loooove to read dictionaries. My nose buried in the dictionary, I didn't see or hear when she began talking to the class. She would then call on me, and I wouldn't hear her. She would continue to try to get my attention from the front of the classroom (I assume—I never saw it) until she got more and more frustrated. She'd wind up coming over to my desk, loudly getting on my case and lecturing me. Every week.
>
> Though it never worked, Mrs. Attitude thought that humiliating me in front of the class would

break me of this terrible habit. I really did hate being yelled at, and I really hated the extra ammo she gave the other kids so that they could increase their taunting on the playground. So I really did try. But handing me a dictionary and telling me not to get absorbed in it was equivalent to leaving an unwrapped Hershey bar on my desk and telling me not to eat it. She assumed that I was driving her nuts on purpose. She seemed to have forgotten what the heck she was teaching. It was a vocabulary lesson! I was reading a dictionary! The fact that she didn't want me to learn new vocabulary words during the vocabulary lesson drove me up the wall!

There were so many ways she could have dealt with this. She could have come over and tapped me on the shoulder before she started talking to the class. She could have set a timer with a loud bell on my desk and told me I had to close the dictionary when it went off. She could have kept me occupied writing definitions on the board while the other kids consulted their dictionaries. She could have coached me to help the other kids with their work. She could have assigned me work that didn't involve a dictionary. She could have ignored the problem and let me read the dictionary. She could have done a lot of things, but she didn't. She humiliated me for a behavior I couldn't control, and she made me loathe and distrust her for making my bullying situation worse.

- Make sure your rewards are true rewards. Being rewarded for good behavior with treats that I hate (hard candy feels awful in my mouth) or toys I don't understand (glad YOU like the *Star Trek* Monopoly game) won't inspire me to change my behavior. My interests are specific, and what gets my attention may be the opposite of what other kids might want. If you want to know what rewards I might like—ask me! If I'm not able to tell you in words, look for other signs that indicate what interests me.

- Choose one behavior at a time to work on. "Multi-tasking" does *not* work for kids with autism.

- Are my behaviors harmful, socially unacceptable, or just annoying? If I'm doing something that affects my health or safety, disrupts the classroom, or makes others avoid me, I understand that you need to help me change that. But then please think about some of my other behaviors that you say are "inappropriate" or "negative." Maybe it bothers some people that I twirl my hair or chew my hoodie string. But of what real importance are those things in the face of all I'm trying to learn and cope with? They're important to *me*; they help me calm myself. Help me change the things (one at a time) that will have the greatest benefit to my being able to learn and be with others comfortably.

- See the big picture, not just me in it. If you always encourage me to be like other children, you may see me emulate some of their less-than-perfect behavior, because I do see and hear the swearing, cheating, and complaining, the sneaky stuff, the teasing and taunting. If you tell me to always tell the truth, don't be surprised if I tell Sophie her hair looks weird. Please be careful what you ask of me when it affects everyone else around us.

So now we have the assignment: behavior doesn't change until we find and address the root cause. Here's the tool kit for doing that.

Functional Behavior Assessment, Functional Behavior Analysis

This is literally the ABC of behavior. It involves identifying the *antecedent*, or trigger, of the *behavior*, the behavior itself that we see the child display, and the *consequence* or result of the behavior. The assessment is part of the analysis. FBA can be anything from informal observation to detailed, quantified data collection. Either is best done alongside a person or persons trained in behavior analysis. Keep in mind the behavior equation we shared at the beginning of the chapter: Behavior = you + me + environment.

Sensory Profile

Occupational therapists (OTs) will be familiar with the Sensory Profile, developed by widely respected OT Winnie Dunn. Parents/caregivers respond to questions regarding the frequency and intensity of their child's responses to a range of sensory experiences. The results are scored by an OT and can be invaluable in pinpointing environmental stimuli that may be contributing to behavior. Information brought to light by the Sensory Profile can also help an OT suggest modifications to the classroom that can help prevent disruptive, resistant, or avoidant behaviors.

Sensory Map/Sensory Diet

With the information gained from the Sensory Profile, an occupational therapist can design a "sensory map" and/or "diet" for the child. The map charts the child's day as she moves from activity to activity, identifies where sensory problems are likely to occur, and provides intervention suggestions, or a diet. For children on the spectrum, the diet may need to include both calming and alerting activities. Disinterest and lethargy (hyposensitive response) can be symptoms of sensory disorder as much as can hyperactivity.

Food Journal

Food can wreak havoc with a child's behavior, far beyond the dismissive, hyped "sugar high." Food allergies (disordered immune system response), food sensitivities (drug-like reaction in degree to varying amounts of a food), low blood sugar, dehydration, vitamin deficiencies, absorption issues—the list is long. Keeping detailed notes on what and when the child eats alongside behavior notes can be quite revealing.

Sleep Journal

Parents may find it invaluable to document the child's sleep habits. Chronic sleep shortage is a potent prescription for behavior troubles. Detecting the source of sleep problems begins with the same factors we've been discussing throughout the chapter: sensory issues such as household noise, uncomfortable bedding or night clothing fabric, smelly (to the child) bath or laundry products. A child with proprioceptive needs might benefit from a weighted blanket or sleeping bag instead of sheets. Some children sleep better with a more defined sleeping space, such as under a bed tent or canopy, or behind a curtain. Television and electronic device activities right up until the moment of bedtime leave the child stimulated, not relaxed. Caffeinated beverages and chocolate products should be avoided in the hours before sleep.

A Clear, Fair, and *Meaningful* Plan for Consequences

Your student's autism may be the reason (explanation or cause) for some of his behaviors, but it can never be the excuse (attempt to justify, perhaps without factual backup). No one would suggest that an autistic child always be spared the natural consequences of his behavior. But the huge qualifier here is: be very clear in making the connection between the behavior and the consequence. Keep your language concrete, backed up by visuals when at all possible.

Jennifer McIlwee Myers again helps us recognize the gravity of this when she says, "We need to understand how our behavior can cause unwanted results for us. DON'T cut us too much slack when our behavior is potentially dangerous to us. For example, adolescent pre-stalking behavior should result in serious consequences—because not treating such behavior seriously when we are young can lead to problems involving law enforcement when we're older."

Eyes and Ears—and Heart

Behaviors rooted in emotional triggers can be the toughest to detect, because your autistic student may not be able to readily identify, let alone articulate, his emotions. We need to listen with our hearts, and listen and look in places we can't easily hear or see. A child experiences many things outside our range of awareness—teasing, bullying, frustration, disappointment, ineptitude at a given task due to lack of ability or knowledge. All of these can erupt into behavior. And most critically—the child with challenged social-emotional and language skills won't be able to communicate what's wrong. The ongoing involvement of a speech language therapist or a mental health professional is highly beneficial. Art, music, or dance therapy can also be considered. Many children can express themselves through drawing, painting, sculpture, or movement when words aren't possible.

If we can buy into the idea that learning is circular, it's only a short step further down the road to realizing that behavior too is circular. Like learning, its messages flow back and forth among the members of the team. Three centuries before the concept of autism emerged, Sir Isaac Newton described the behavior equation perfectly in his Third Law of Motion: for every action, there's an equal and opposite

71

reaction. This kind of built-up pressure is what launches that all-time favorite science project, the bottle rocket. Behavior issues can seem about that volatile! But you have control of this rocket's trajectory. Your words, your attitude, your actions, and your reactions are determining factors in your student's environment and his response to it. Only when we take a clear-eyed look at our own behavior will we have a chance of positively impacting our children's.

Chapter Five

Glitched, Garbled, and Bewildered

If we can't communicate effectively,
neither of us will learn much.

"Suppose you say that I said that she said something quite different; I don't see that it makes any difference, because if she said what you said I said she said, it's just the same as if I said what she said she said."

> — Slow-Solid Turtle to Painted Jaguar in Rudyard Kipling's "The Beginning of the Armadillos"

Perhaps you were perplexed by the previous page, with its blank expanse. Maybe you wondered if there had been some sort of printing error. But what if I told you there was no printing error, that there was a message on that page; that, in fact, the white space contained a blizzard of information, but that you simply weren't getting it? What if, as the author of this book, in effect the teacher, I chose to send the information in a form other than conventional words, a form that's perfectly understandable to me but not to you? Or what if I chose to write this entire chapter in the Kipling-style double-speak quoted above? Chances are you would feel annoyed, possibly frustrated, maybe even angry. Isn't it my responsibility as the teacher to provide information in a manner you can comprehend?

The answer is a resounding OF COURSE IT IS. We have the responsibility and the obligation as teachers to do whatever is necessary to communicate effectively with all of our students. We may think we are, but the assumptions and expectations we carry as "regular" communicators can fall far short of the mark with our autistic student. Too often, we unknowingly but insidiously sabotage our efforts and theirs.

This is inarguable: the student with autism *requires adaptive communication*. Many teachers are aware that children on the spectrum are more often than not visual learners and that they interpret language in a literal manner. I addressed those two aspects of autism at length in my book *Ten Things Every Child with Autism Wishes You Knew* (third edition, 2019), and here I'll extend that discussion rather than repeat it.

Recognizing that our student is a visual learner and concrete thinker is the tip of the iceberg. Like an iceberg, the characteristic language issues of autism go far below the surface, and they make auditory language processing both treacherous and genuinely exhausting for him. Surrounded by mainstream contemporary conversation, our student is subjected to an impossible level of vocabulary, relentless use of vernacular, idiom, or just plain, I mean, like, ya know, sloppy use of the language and stuff, ROFL! Layer on top of that the ephemeral nuances of language: vocal pitch, tone, volume and the sheer pace of talk (human and electronic) flying around your autistic student, and it becomes so indecipherable as to send him into self-defensive shutdown. It looks to you like he's not listening, but the reality is that *he* is desperately trying to comprehend but we aren't communicating in a manner that makes sense to him.

Having to battle each day through a fog of what may sound to him like jabberwocky doesn't encourage our student to trust us as messengers. When communication falters or fails, so too goes his trust. And that trust is the glue that binds your relationship as teacher and learner.

> "I don't believe you!" said Painted Jaguar. "You've mixed up all the things (you) told me to do until I don't know whether I am on my head or my painted tail. And now you come and tell me something I can understand, and I don't trust you one little bit."

We may already be using some form of visual schedule, choice board, or sign language for our student. We may have noticed their literal interpretation of language, maybe even find it somewhat amusing.

> Well-meaning neighbor: "My goodness, Justin, you're growing like a weed!"
>
> Justin: "You're a mean old man! My daddy pulls weeds and throws them away!"

That story came to me from a real mom, and I have a thousand of my own like it. These incidents are humorous only in the moment, and not at all when you consider that unchecked concrete thinking can lead to a lifetime of misinterpreting neighbors, co-workers, and family members. How will that impact a child's ability to function as a happy, independent adult? So much of the general population, even those who spend a lot of time around autistic individuals, remain unaware of how deeply disadvantaged our autistic student is in the area of communication, and how acutely aware of this we need to become to teach him effectively.

An interesting culinary movement called Slow Food arose in the late 20th century. One of its goals was to counteract the growing pervasiveness of empty-calorie, low-nutrient fast food and to reawaken connection between people and cultures. I'd love to see a similar movement applied to the use of language in communicating with our students with autism.

Slow down if you want to cultivate healthy communication with him. Move closer, speak to him directly (not calling from across the room), use low but intelligible tones, and check the speed of your speech. *Slow down.*

Cut out the fat. This includes empty-calorie, low-nutrient verbiage such as slang, inference, sarcasm, allusion, exaggeration, cute but unnecessary plays on words. For your student, these embellishments serve only to clutter and obscure, not enhance, the core message you're trying to put across. Use concrete, specific language.

Balance the diet. Just as any one food is not complete nutrition, words alone are only one component of communication. Put all the team heads together to determine the types of visual, aural, tactile, kinesthetic, and social-emotional supports he needs. Actively teach him to understand body language, facial expression, vocal nuances, proxemics. He won't simply pick it up through social osmosis as he goes along. It requires perpetual integration. Every teacher, every setting, every day.

Give him adequate time to digest. It takes him longer to process and formulate the proper words to respond and to motor plan the attendant behavior needed. Motor planning is the term for how we formulate and sequence action steps in our mind before attempting to perform a task. It's a learned ability that grows out of the sensory integration development process, and many students with autism become quite adept at it. *Slow down.* When speaking with or to him, wait—many beats—for him to respond before jumping in. Too often, we ask this child to pay the price for our own lack of time management skills. That's not okay. If his communication software calls for a fifteen-second pause before responding or for a five-minute warning or two-minute warning before an activity changes, build in that extra time on your end, because this is his processor's system requirement.

Let him stop when he's full. Continuing to force-feed information past the point where he's able to adequately absorb it will only send his system into overload. As a result, you'll see a blow-out or a shutdown—either way, a "work stoppage."

Functional Communication:
Mission Essential

The importance of providing a child with a functional communication system, *in whatever form it may take*, cannot be over-emphasized. When I speak to groups, I put my audience through an exercise simulating what it might be like to lose their own chosen means of functional communication. It goes like this:

Envision having to navigate your day with your mouth taped shut and your fingers taped together. No phone, no email, no texting, no social media. Your ability to contribute to conversations

The importance of providing a child with a functional communication system, *in whatever form it may take*, cannot be over-emphasized.

both oral and digital is severely compromised, as is your ability to ask for clarification of information that has whizzed by too quickly. It requires physical effort and exponentially more time to offer an opinion, ask for assistance, and make your needs and wants known. You can't use the phone to summon help or expedite your tasks.

Imagine further that any printed information handed to you is written in symbols you don't fully understand. Verbal information is coming at you as if in a foreign language; you can only pick out every sixth word and maybe the ending verb—and that's only when the speaker slows down the pace of his speech, enunciates clearly, and speaks to you directly.

With no functional communication as you know it, imagine trying to do your job, fulfill your responsibilities, and meet the expectations of family, coworkers, and community. Then ask yourself:

How effective would I be?

How successful would I be?

How would my co-workers and family members react?

How much could I contribute?

How long before my frustration, anxiety, anger, and fear boiled over and forced me to exhibit some "behavior?"

And what if this went on, day after day, not an experiment that ended after a few hours? What is this was my *life*?

By the time I've asked our gathering to imagine all this, the room always gets very quiet.

And in imagining this, I hope you can begin to feel the great urgency and great poignancy in your ASD student's circumstance: language and communication is only one vital area of their lives with which they're struggling.

For nonspeaking children and for emerging speakers, talk *is* cheap. Alternate and/or supplemental forms of communication are mandatory. Even for children with autism who present as speech-competent, you can be certain of this: there are *always* holes and discrepancies, and they're deeper than you imagine. Even when my son was a teenager and presenting as more language-capable than he actually was, the extraordinary effort required of him and the toll exacted to execute competent social communication was palpable and frequently heart-wrenching to have to watch.

Nobody saw me cry. Certainly not him.

As a society, we find it too easy to ignore or marginalize those who can't speak up for themselves until they do something extreme that gets our attention. If we fail to provide a child with functional means of expressing their needs, we have no right to be shocked or exasperated when they melt down in anger, frustration, or grief. And it isn't enough that we provide them the means in finite settings. It must be a go-everywhere-they-do solution. The large visual schedule on the wall in the classroom is very useful, as is the choice board at home, but what happens in the myriad venues outside the classroom and the home? The solution must be portable, something the child can use across all the landscapes where his life is unfolding. Digital applications have made this portability more widely, but by no means universally, available. Nor are electronic devices and applications infallible, nor are they invulnerable to damage, theft, and dead batteries. As with communication itself, the functional solution must be multi-pronged.

Speech Is Not Language Is Not Communication

The ability to speak, to form words, is only the mechanical beginning of verbal communication. Forming words is a function of the articulator muscles of the lips, tongue, and face. Here's an analogy: you can switch on the ignition of a car and the engine will run, but without your steering and direction, an idling motor goes nowhere. At that point, it's a car but it's not yet transportation.

Merely using spoken words doesn't equate to having a command of functional language, nor does *not* using spoken words mean that communication isn't possible. The term *nonverbal* has been widely used to characterize people who don't speak, but it's not an accurate use of the word, and the distinction between nonverbal and nonspeaking is significant. Nonverbal means not using words as a mode of communication. Nonspeaking means not using spoken words as a means of communication. Nonspeaking people often have a deep grasp of language and use words to communicate in a range of written modes, or audio modes made possible by assistive technology.

Functional language comprises receptive language (understanding what's being communicated to us) and expressive language (ability to make ourselves understood), all with the overarching umbrella of social pragmatics. Functional language isn't just words we say and hear, but how we say and hear them, when, where, and to whom we say them and why we say them.

It's understandable that as verbal, speaking people ourselves, we tend to focus strongly on getting kids to talk. For parents of children who don't talk, it's sometimes a primary goal. And yet, addressing the problem indirectly may be the shortest path, even if it seems counter-intuitive. When I met New Hampshire physical therapist Patti Rawding-Anderson, she was offering social communication groups for children on the autism spectrum. She described to me how parents worry that if they give their nonspeaking child sign language or a picture system, the child will have no motivation to learn to talk. "But getting them to engage in their world is the most important thing," she says. "If you give them an augmentative communication system—a picture exchange system (PECS) is one example—or anything that allows them a sense of exploration and independence, and a *fun* way to be successful, you'll find that functional communication will follow."

Keep It Concrete: Say What You Mean; Mean What You Say

In the United States, use of the English language over the last few decades has gotten sloppier by the day. It's a wonder that children with autism can understand us at all. They're forced to dodge language sinkholes every step of their day:

- Listen to any casual conversation and count the number of times you hear "And I'm like..." when what the speaker means is "And I said... or "And then he goes, like..." instead of "And then he said..." The child with autism is thinking, *he goes? Where did he go?*

- Listen to your own language. Is it littered with frightening phrasal verbs and idioms like cutting in on someone, breaking up with someone, burning through his homework, getting kicked out of class, putting a bug in someone's ear, opening a can of worms, suggesting that your restless student has ants in his pants?

- Do you assume your student understands homophones? Don't. Did he bat (verb) the bat (flying mammal) with the bat (baseball equipment)? Did the light from the light-yellow moon make it appear lighter than air?

- And then there's nonspecific speech. It's not fair to tell this student to "Go get it," with a glance over your shoulder, and expect him to understand that what you mean is, "Use the atlas on the top shelf to look up the capital of Montana."

- Your autistic student struggles with social inferencing. "You didn't turn your homework in" is merely a statement of fact to her. She doesn't understand you're waiting for an explanation from her, or for her to produce the homework. She needs to hear your directive in the positive rather than the imperative: "Please put your spelling sentences homework on my desk." Don't make her guess or have to figure out what it is you want her to do. That's setting her up for failure.

At this point you may find yourself thinking how grueling it will be to have to police your language to such a degree to communicate with your autistic student. Now you begin to get some inkling of how debilitating it is for her to have to deal with a whole world full of bullet-train chatterboxes who, to her, are alternating between gobbledygook and gibberish.

Be Clear about What You Are Trying to Teach— and Teach Only One Thing at a Time

Check your teaching materials against the challenges of autism and you may find that they often confuse rather than define or clarify, making it impossible to determine exactly what the student does or doesn't know.

Your student's need for concrete expression extends into the realm of words on paper. The print language they confront in textbooks, teaching materials, and tests can confound them every bit as much as the verbal chatter they hear. The following passage, adapted from my book *The Autism Trail Guide: Postcards from the Road Less Traveled*, gives stark example:

As the parent of a student with autism, I've become wary of anything with the word *standardized* in front of it. Standardized tests, lessons, and worksheets—most require modification to be appropriate for a child with autism. "Math Suks!" warbles Jimmy Buffett's famous song. My son Bryce might agree, except upon closer examination, it's probably not math that "suks," but the confusing language in which it's sometimes presented and from which he's expected to learn.

Here's an example of how a standard math worksheet constitutes a morass of ambiguity for the student with autism. It will be an eye-opener to those who don't realize the depth and breadth of the language difficulties faced by so many autistic students. The example comes from an actual worksheet Bryce received on the first day of school one year. It nearly paralyzed him, and not because he couldn't add and subtract. He was fully competent at that. But with his moderate-to-severe challenges in vocabulary, inferential ability, and generalization skills, the worksheet, labeled as a Grade 5 math sheet but using language several grade levels higher, was a minefield of unnecessary and unclear language that made it impossible to gauge his true math competence.

Addition and Subtraction

Directions: Add or subtract to find the answers.

Problem 1: Eastland School hosted a field day. Students could sign up for a variety of events. 175 students signed up for individual races. Twenty two-person teams competed in the mile relay and 36 kids took part in the high jump. How many students participated in the activities?

- "Students could sign up for a variety of events": unnecessary, irrelevant information.

- "Twenty two-person teams." Bryce read this, as many ASD students would, without the hyphen: 22, not 20 x 2. The directions tell him to "add or subtract to find the answer," but the text shifts in mid-problem and requires multiplication within the add-or-subtract operation. Unclear, inconsistent directions are nearly impossible for many ASD kids to follow.

- We don't know how many students "participated" because some "competed" and some "took part," but some only "signed up."

- The worksheet is labeled Grade 5, but the Flesch-Kincaid Readability test rates this problem as Grade 9.

The same problem rewritten in an autism-friendly manner that emphasizes math, not language, might read:

At Eastland School field day, 175 students ran in individual races. Forty students ran in a relay race, and 36 kids did the high jump. How many students participated in field day?

Problem 2: Each school was awarded a trophy for participating in the field day activities. The Booster Club planned to purchase three plaques as awards, but they only wanted to spend $150. The first-place trophy they selected was $68. The second-place award was $59. How much would they be able to spend on the third-place award if they stay within their budgeted amount?

- In the first sentence, reference is made to a "trophy." In the next sentence, it changes to "plaque," then it's back to "trophy" and in the fourth sentence it becomes an "award." All are referring to the same thing, but the math problem has now become an exercise in knowledge of synonyms, obscuring the math intent.

- Problem assumes an eighth-grade vocabulary. How many children know what a "Booster Club" is? A club for people who need baby seats in restaurants?

Autism friendly wording: A group of parents had $150 with which to buy trophies for the teams finishing first, second, and third place. The first-place trophy they selected was $68. The second-place trophy was $59. How much money was left to spend on the third-place trophy?

For the child with autism, these problems don't assess math skills; they evaluate ability to decode the language of a poorly written standardized worksheet designed for a general population, one written at several grade levels above both the student's chronological age and even the purported grade level of the worksheet itself.

Teachers, I want you to know that I fully realize that, even when you're able to comprehend the magnitude of this problem, figuring out what to do about it may seem overwhelming. After one such session with one of my favorite teachers, she said: "I completely understand what you're telling me about the fact that he thinks differently. To accommodate that, I can see that I would have to go through all my materials and revamp everything for him. Frankly, I don't see how I can manage that—I have 150 students. What can we do?"

Her approach was the right one: teamwork in action. She acknowledged a large and genuine problem, and I acknowledged the large and genuine constraints on her time. Her suggested solution was to pull Bryce into a three-way meeting and let him know that homework was to be interpreted by the spirit, not the letter of the assignment, and that she was giving permission for Mom to be the arbiter of that. We could write, we could discuss, we could draw, we could look at the internet—whatever made the information comprehensible to him, and I would sign off on what we'd done. This approach had the added advantage of encouraging Bryce to think flexibly, and many times that was more difficult—and more useful—than the assignment itself. On the other end, she modified her assessment methods to ensure that he was able to communicate what he knew. Along the way, the school speech therapist would step in with particularly difficult assignments, using her sessions with Bryce to break things down into understandable pieces.

You may end up thanking your autistic student for pushing you to examine your written materials more closely. We may go along for quite a while using materials we think are working until one day we get startling evidence that they aren't. I'm thinking of a social studies worksheet we encountered asking students to locate the USSR—on a 21st-century map. Bryce knocked himself to bits trying to find a republic that had already ceased to exist before he was born. Assuming a level of prior knowledge—that he would know that the bulk of the former USSR is now called Russia—is as unfair (to any student!) as are poorly written materials.

Beyond Words

By focusing so heavily on the spoken components of communication, it's easy to overlook the less concrete aspects of social communication that are admittedly harder to teach. Because our students on the spectrum experience language in its most concrete form, they need a great deal of guidance and an even greater amount of practice to move beyond their concept of using language merely as a tool to obtain information or get needs met. The vast scope of *communicative intent* isn't automatically present in the consciousness of autistic children. These complicated facets of communication go far beyond diction and vocabulary: that people use words to comfort, to praise, to entertain, but also to provoke fear, shame, and trickery.

At age three, my son Connor would burst into his grandparents' house with the greeting, "B-i-i-i-g TRUCKS!" At age four, Bryce's standard greeting was "I've got a dinosaur!" Their preschool teachers, by example and gentle daily guidance, instilled in them that we say "Good morning" when we come into class or see someone for the first time that day. That's the beginning of social pragmatics—the social use of language—and for the student with autism, it only gets even more complicated. Asking, greeting, negotiating, protesting, instructing—these tend to be verbal tasks or expectations. Beyond that level lies the realm of nuance, inference, and nonverbal communication with all its explosive potential for misinterpretation and social misery.

There are three broad categories of social communication, all of which are minefields for your autistic student.

Vocalic communication: She doesn't recognize the nuances of spoken language: sarcasm, puns, idioms, hints, slang, abstraction. She may speak in a monotone or may speak too loudly, too softly, too quickly, or too slowly.

Kinesthetic communication: She doesn't understand body language, facial expression, or emotional responses (crying, recoiling). She may use gestures or postures inappropriately or miss the communicative intent of eye contact.

Proxemic communication: She doesn't understand physical space communication, the subtle territorial norms of personal boundaries. She may be an unwitting "space invader." The rules of proxemics not only vary from culture to culture, but from person to person depending upon relationship: Intimate? Casual but personal? Social only? Public space? For many kids with ASDs, deciphering proxemics requires an often impossible level of inference.

Student See, Student Do

Your visually oriented student depends on you to model the kinds of behaviors and responses you want to see in her. Show, in addition to telling her, what you expect of her, and do it repeatedly and patiently in a manner that makes sense to her.

And above all, show her basic respect. When she's angry, distraught, in discomfort, or emotionally or sensorily overwhelmed, she's not going to be receptive to teaching. Would you be, even as an adult? If during these moments we employ raised voices, scorn, annoyance, mockery, accusation and/or castigation, the only thing we'll be teaching her about functional communication is that language can be wielded to inflict hurt.

Teaching this daunting but rich complexity of language and communication can't be laid solely in the lap of a speech therapist (should the student be fortunate enough to have such services). Nor can we compartmentalize the teaching of language skills separate from social skills. They're inseparable and omnipresent, and this means that there is challenge in every waking moment, yes, but also opportunity present at every turn in every situation. The teaching of functional language calls for an ensemble effort, every teacher in the child's circle of learning working to move the student toward a life-changing goal: achieving the understanding that language in its most basic form will do more than simply get her needs met. In its most glorious and elevated form, it will give her the power to define herself as she wants others to see her and to stake claim to the place she rightfully wants to occupy in the world.

Chapter Six

Teach the Whole Me

I'm much more than a set of broken pieces or missing parts.

"The whole is more than the sum of its parts."

Most of us recognize Aristotle's famous truism. But he went on to say more: that "educating the mind without educating the heart is no education at all." Aristotle, both philosopher and scientist, understood this inescapable connectedness between all the parts of ourselves. Within that interconnectedness lies the potential for either soaring harmony or soul-shattering discord, depending on how each part works in relation to the others.

And, "parts" is too often how some view our autistic students. We focus on the symptoms or characteristics of autism to such a degree that we lose sight of the child as a holistic being. A child with autism isn't a malfunctioning engine to be parted out and repaired, with the speech therapist fixing the talking part and the sensory and fine motor part going to the occupational therapist. A physical therapist deals with the gross motor part. This part goes to the behavior specialist and that part to the psychologist and the dietician, and so on. All these disciplines are invaluable pieces of the whole puzzle. But unless actively integrated with each other, they can actually escalate the obstacles we're striving to remove. "We should not 'therapize' children," says Patti Rawding-Anderson, "filling their world with adults who're all trying to do something to them. What message does this send the child? More important than therapy, language and cognition is to help the child see the inter-relatedness of the people in his life, and build upon those relationships across various situations. If a child feels connected, he will have the internal motivation he needs to pursue the other things."

We should not therapize children. It's more important to help the child see the inter-relatedness of the people in his life, and build upon those relationships.

When we don't create that connectedness for the child, one of the gravest risks we run is mistaking compliance for learning. You can get a child to perform certain behaviors or bring forth certain words in certain situations. But without addressing the core reasons for the original behaviors, or conveying the function and utility of language and communication, the child is still without meaningful context. And context is everything.

We've already looked at how speech is only one of the many building blocks of communication, rote repetition of manners doesn't equate to social understanding, and attempting to change behavior without looking at underlying biomedical, sensory, or emotional triggers simply isn't looking at the whole picture. It therefore will never be a whole answer, never result in a whole child or an adult being able to do much more than go through the motions of social expectation. You may have put out the fire, but in its place are opaque puddles.

How successful we are in teaching the whole child has a lot to do with our own personal culture of disability. Service providers like Patti Rawding-Anderson work with a wide spectrum of families and teachers, and these professionals tell you it's almost eerie how individuals who come to them for help sift into two camps. Ask these two camps the same question: what would you like me to know about your student or child? In the first camp are teachers and parents who

All human beings have innate personalities; your student also has aspects of her individuality that manifest apart from her autism.

say: "This child is so bright and energetic! He loves the outdoors and he has a lot of knowledge in his head. How can we help him settle and focus better so he and his classmates can enjoy each other?" From the second camp, we hear: "This child is disruptive and inattentive. He's always making noise, making messes, getting out of his seat, and talking out of turn. He needs to get himself under control."

It's clear which of these attitudes is more whole-child, which teacher is going to build the more successful teacher-child relationship, and which teacher's student is going to be the more successful learner and ultimately the more successful adult.

We've already acknowledged the complexity and spectrum nature of autism. It may be easier to see the whole child in your autistic student if we look beyond what autism is to look equally hard at what autism isn't.

- **Not everything she does is a result of her autism.** All human beings have innate personalities; your student also has aspects of her individuality that manifest apart from her autism. Children with autism aren't the only ones who shave the kitty or eat dog food on a dare while refusing "real" food. Her devout passion for running, reading, entomology, or air fryers isn't necessarily autism-driven. Both are aspects of a developing child who's pushing boundaries on one hand and discovering her own assets on another hand. Autism may affect the degree to which these behaviors manifest but isn't always the reason for them.

- **Natural typical development will be happening as well.** During his school years from pre-K through elementary school, Bryce earned a consistent reputation as a cheerful, tireless workhorse. So I was surprised when a middle school teacher told me, not unkindly, that he "fusses and complains all the time." When I repeated the "compliment" to him at home, he beamed and replied, "Yes, I do! I'm a teenager!"

The teacher knew that his behavior was part of adolescence, not autism. It's also not unusual that a teenager might care more about a peer's opinion of him than he would a teacher's. A more subdued Bryce came home shortly after the fussing-and-complaining conversation and asked me if I remembered Jessie (not her real name), an elementary school classmate whose family had moved away a few years back. I did remember her as a nice girl, so I was happy for Bryce when he told me she'd moved back to town and was again in some of his classes. He hesitated a beat, then told me: "She says I've changed. She says I used to be nice but now I'm kind of grumpy." Did he think this was true? "Yes," he admitted, "I guess it is sometimes." But I could see the wheels turning. Maybe the stereotypical grumpy teenager is an amusing way to treat a teacher. But maybe it isn't

94

the best persona to present to a friendly peer. Shortly after this incident, the good-natured Bryce returned.

As his teacher: Emphasize commonalities, not just differences that many children with autism share with their peers.

Emphasize commonalities, not just differences that many children with autism share with their peers.

- They have dreams for the future. Most aspire to many of the usual facets of adult independence—interesting work, home and money of their own, a social circle that works for them. Many will drive, vote, live with a spouse or partner, become parents.

- They enjoy humor and fun. If you think your autistic student has no sense of humor, consider how subjective humor is. Americans sometimes think British humor odd, and vice versa. Older folks often aren't amused by humor that appeals to younger folks. The joke that entertains some mortally offends others. Humor is in the eye of the beholder. Your student assuredly has a sense of humor. It may not be the same as yours or his peers. What a great opportunity to consider another perspective!

- They can and will be friendly and sociable—in their own, appropriately calibrated way. The spring pep rally or the crush of the Halloween parade may send your autistic student into sensory overload, but the three-person Lego Club group or a two-person sandcastle team may be just right.

- They can belong. It's a matter of tailoring the setting. Team expectations such as baseball, basketball, lines in a play, or a band solo may overwhelm, but there are many ways to be part of a team without the undue all-eyes-on-you pressure of personal performance. Swim and track teams are generally more personal-best-oriented than group team sports. Singing in the choir, painting the scenery for the class play, or taking photos at school events are endeavors that can be enjoyable for all-comers. Volunteer opportunities at places like pet shelters and food banks draw the child into a larger world.

- They have feelings. Having open communication with an autistic child about feelings and emotions can be difficult. Conversation in general can be difficult for them, and more so can their ability to identify and articulate emotions for which they may not yet have the vocabulary to describe (even if the adults around them think they should). That they may not be able to show or communicate their feelings doesn't mean that they don't experience the full galaxy of human emotions. If we're to be able to help them recognize, empathize, and identify the feelings of others, it must start with our validating that the same feelings live within them.

- They want to be liked and have friends—as does most everyone. If you've ever yearned to do or learn something but simply didn't know where to start, you'll understand where the child with autism stands. Social communication requires an intricate set of skills. Many students on the spectrum haven't been taught these skills and hence don't have them—which is in no way the same as not wanting to have them.

As his teacher: Recognize when outside help or a fresh approach is needed, or when the school or teacher, hard as they may have tried (or not), simply isn't a good fit. This is where it's incumbent upon the team to look at the whole child in the whole picture, remove egos and should-haves from the equation, and make decisions that are in the best interests of the child.

In a culture where we're constantly pummeled to "Never give up!", stepping back from that ego can be hard. Happily, I have by now had enough firsthand experience doing it that I can see the value and the remarkable end results of letting go. Acknowledging when a team member or particular program or approach can't provide the appropriate and necessary services for this particular student isn't failure—it's the very essence of putting the needs of the child first. When done in the true spirit of wanting the child to succeed, it's courageous. "Never give up?" As we considered back in Chapter Two, life on the autism spectrum sometimes dictates that the stronger and wiser response is "Let go or be dragged."

Letting someone with a better skill set and a clean slate (no history of failure) tackle the situation can be just the ticket. I went through a years-long, painfully unsuccessful process of trying to teach Bryce to ride a bike. It turned out to be a microcosm for many whole-child learning lessons, and we'll explore that further in Chapter Nine. But here, I can tell you that the happy ending to the story had everything to do with my conceding that I wasn't the right one to teach this skill and that the harder I tried, the more it didn't happen. Our adapted PE teacher, Sarah Spella, volunteered to take over the job—and accomplished it in under an hour.

The critical component was my being able to let go of ego. Maybe I should have been able to teach Bryce to ride a bike myself—I had taught his brother at what I thought was a usual age. But with Bryce, I had reached the point where accepting outside help was the only scenario that made sense. My failure wouldn't be in my lack of success in teaching him to ride the bike; it would be in neglecting to look beyond my ego for the resources to achieve the goal.

It takes courage and initiative, says Sarah, to be able to say, "I think my student or child can do this, but I'm not the right one to teach him. I may not be teaching him the way that he needs to be taught."

Bryce learned to ride a bike because every subconscious expectation had been removed. Alone in the gym with Sarah, he was away from the prying eyes of neighborhood children who might snicker at his training wheels, away from a parent who he knew had successfully taught an older sibling at a younger age, away from the specter of the other bikes in the garage poised for the annual vacation, away from having to worry about "being brave" if he fell.

"Be aware of how much information kids get about themselves from their environment," Sarah told me. The measuring stick is never far from a child, whether in the form of a spoken expectation, "Keep trying!" or those unspoken expectations all around them, like seeing younger children do what they cannot yet. As teachers and parent-teachers, part of our job is to recognize how the educational setting is affecting the child, how it may be impeding learning and when it's time for a change.

Respecting your ASD student as a complex but complete self must be a concept as circular as all the others we discuss in this book: whole child, whole teacher. Accept and respect your own developmental timeline. "We think about the developmental sequence for the child," says Patti Rawding-Anderson, "but parents (and professionals) go through a developmental sequence too. You're not born with the skills and knowledge to parent or teach a child who has challenges. It's a parallel process you follow with the child. Too many 'systems' don't take this into account—the need to nurture your own development as you build a relationship with the whole child."

The whole is more than the sum of its parts. Today we have a new word for Aristotle's axiom: synergy, from the Greek word *sunergos*, meaning "working together." Only when we take to heart and put into practice this 2,300-year-old-wisdom will we truly be able to say that we have left no part of this child behind.

Chapter Seven

Be Curious

...be very curious.

"Curiosity is the very basis of education and if you tell me that curiosity killed the cat, I say only the cat died nobly."

— Arnold Edinborough

A mid several thousand years' worth of knowledge that humankind has amassed about the workings of the human brain, autism is quite the new kid on the block. The word *autism* didn't exist before the work of Dr. Leo Kanner in 1943. We can all admit that there are aspects of autism yet a puzzlement to us. We can also admit that each of us confronts that which we don't understand in our own way. Some people embrace the unknown as collective potential—a means to knowledge and an exciting challenge. Others will avoid such mystery, seeing it as intimidating chaos.

I'm thinking that most who choose to become teachers gravitate toward the first group: lifelong learners, knowledge-seekers comfortable with taking a certain amount of risk. Most teachers I know would look at their autistic students with a real desire to reach this sometimes-enigmatic child and have a positive impact on his life. We parents might tell our best teachers that they lit a (metaphorical) fire under our child. But how do you strike the spark for a child who outwardly seems remote, detached—unknowable?

In your role as firestarter, and for your student and you as a team, curiosity is both the flint and the fuel. Inquisitive thinking, that endlessly questioning spirit, forms the basis of all human progress. "Inquiring minds want to know!" blares the old tabloid newspaper ad. Most young children embrace this. They ask and ask and ask about their world, sometimes wearing us out with their questions (as it should be). The more curious of my two kids asked me, do farts weigh anything? The lady's tummy is round because she has a baby growing inside her? How did she swallow the baby? How come people don't fall off the bottom of the world? If an orange is called an orange, why isn't a banana called a yellow? If the shampoo is green or purple or orange, why are the bubbles always white? Is a skeleton a person?

Did you know that Albert Einstein said, "It is a miracle that curiosity survives formal education"? If I were an educator, I would *dive* to pick up that gauntlet. But your autistic student may never have had that typical child-curiosity to lose. The exercise of curiosity can require risk-taking, that figurative stepping off the path, trading what you have in hand for what's as yet unseen, unknown. That's too tall an order for some autistic students; the world they experience may be literally (given sensory dysfunction) and figuratively too uneven to consider such boldness.

Typically developing non-autistic young children with emerging self-reliance are freer to indulge their naturally curious natures. Unencumbered by the hell of half a dozen disordered sensory modalities, effortlessly processing the simultaneous inputs that come their way, and able to relate to people who think more or less like they do, they find many of their experiences stimulating, fun, or useful. They're able to roll with little nicks and bruises to knees and feelings because the balance is in their favor. The return they get for their investment in curiosity pays worthwhile dividends.

I've already suggested in this book, and let there be no question about it, that for your student with autism, the world is often not a delightful place. Although she may gather encyclopedic knowledge in one or two interest areas, there may be no general sense of wondering or questioning that drives her to want to explore every little new animal, mineral, or vegetable that crosses her path. For her,

Without a foundation of curiosity, her world will remain without that shower of cerebral sparks that makes learning such a dynamic experience.

the balance may not skew toward positive experiences. She's working hard just to stay upright and put one foot in front of the other on a slender path already booby-trapped with tree roots and potholes. Too often, new experiences defeat rather than reward her. Be curious? she says. There's more than enough already pulling and pushing me off balance as it is. Why would I volunteer for more turmoil?

For this student, the art of asking questions may come only after sustained encouragement and practice. Especially difficult will be the "I wonder" questions which demand so much more of her than a factual response. But without a foundation of curiosity, her world will remain two-dimensional and without that figurative shower of cerebral sparks that makes learning such a dynamic experience, over and over again. More than ever, she needs for you to invoke all that led you to become a teacher in the first place—to instill the thrill of discovery, to become utterly bewitched by the vastness of knowledge and all the possibility it embodies.

When Bryce was very young, I couldn't even coax him to be curious about Curious George. He rejected not only George but nearly all children's books, and that made me intensely curious and determined to find the inroad. Eventually I did—he didn't like stories about anthropomorphic animals or adults behaving badly (he later deemed—literally and correctly—The Man in the Yellow to be a poacher and a negligent parent, always leaving George alone in situations where he was sure to get in trouble). Bryce wanted stories about human kids, or animals behaving in natural ways, illustrated with photographs rather than abstract art.

It took a heroic amount of curiosity-driven trial-and-error, but I learned to stir his curiosity about new experiences by going in through the back door of his interest areas. He resisted our annual trips to the apple orchards until I told him he could soak himself in the rotary-head sprinklers (he loved any kind of water play) or he could splat the fallen rotten apples against the tree trunks (made cool sounds and looked like barf). Score!

Ultimately, his potentially traumatic transition to middle school was smooth as butter—because he had a teacher who was inherently curious. This teacher said, "I want to connect with him. I'd like him to make me a list of every movie he's ever seen, so we can talk about all kinds of topics. And please tell me, what has worked for him in the past? What hasn't worked for him in the past? Tell me anything about him that you think is important for me to know."

It does take effort and initiative to be curious enough to step inside the autism way of thinking and processing to see what might make your student curious. The job will be easier if you wipe your slate clean of any and all preconceived assumptions you may harbor about your student, perhaps not even consciously. Never assume anything! Assumptions without facts behind them are only guesses, and preconceived notions will squash both your curiosity and your student's as surely as the famous short film *Bambi vs. Godzilla*. An old proverb tells us, "Who shall kindle others must himself glow." To kindle curiosity:

- *Remember* that autism is an open-ended equation, one that should never end with our deciding that the child has reached "the extent of his capability."

- *Forget* using teaching tactics not aligned with the student's brain processing and learning style: *wonder* how well strategies you've always used with non-autistic students will fare within the structure of autism. Be willing to change up what you've always done.

- *Remember* that teaching this uncurious child the love of learning itself is far more imperative than any facts you may want him to learn.

- *Forget* comparisons to other students, even other autistic students. This one occupies his own singular spot on the autism spectrum.

> *Remember* that autism is an open-ended equation, one that should never end with our deciding that the child has reached "the extent of his capability."

In urging us to be curious and assume nothing, our child can illuminate the hundreds of ways in which we might go awry with seemingly benign assumptions:

If you don't get why I don't get it, ask "I wonder... ?" I may not know or understand the rules or the reason for the rule. Am I breaking the rule because there's an underlying cause? I know I'm not supposed to get out of my seat without permission, but maybe I've tried and tried to get your attention and failed. Are your rules contradictory? We aren't supposed to eat in class, but you hand out candy when we do well on the spelling test, so why can't I get my apple out of my backpack?

I may have heard your instructions but not understood them. Or maybe I knew it yesterday but can't retrieve it today. My rote memory is great, but my ability to recall random information, not good. Are you sure I know how to do what you are asking of me? Do you ever wonder why I suddenly need to run to the bathroom every time I'm asked to do a math exercise? Maybe I don't know how or fear my effort will not be good enough or don't know how to ask for help or just can't face more embarrassment in front of my classmates. I need you to stick with me through as many repetitions of tasks and skills as it takes until I feel capable. I can learn and I will learn, but I need more practice than other kids.

I know you want me to learn facts and skills, but before I can do that, I need to learn to become comfortable with the process of learning itself.

And if you don't know all the answers to my questions or to questions about me, it sets a great example for me if you say, "I don't know, but I'll find out." I'm told that asking for help from someone who knows more than me is the mark of a smart student. So wouldn't it be the mark of a smart teacher too?

Tap into your old childhood skills. Ask and ask and ask—ask the occupational therapist, even if the problem doesn't appear to be sensory or motor-related. Ask the speech pathologist, even if it doesn't appear to be language-related (one speech therapist told me that for as many as 80 percent of children identified with learning disabilities, those difficulties are language-based). Ask your student himself, even if you think he won't be able to give you the answers. Ask him by reversing the original question or framing the question as true-or-false, and let him answer in any mode meaningful to him. *Be curious* enough to ask classmates and siblings, because you don't know what goes on in the restroom, the locker room, the back bedroom, the back yard, and every other nook in this wide world where the child is out of adult earshot and line of vision, and the insights of a child may be striking. Ask the "I wonder" questions, and ask them of the range of professionals, paraprofessionals, family members, caregivers, and peers. Here's where circular learning can rise to its highest level and where teamwork is at its most effective.

"I wonder...?" Such an empowering approach, suggesting so much more possibility than merely asking "why?" Can't you just picture our child and his reading partner, whether teacher or family member or peer, with their books and their wonderings—cohorts in learning, gently pushing boundaries? It's so telling, and so appropriate, that the word *wonder* has two meanings: 1) to question, and 2) to marvel.

Chapter Eight

Can I Trust You?

Champions and advocates come in persuasions as varied as the human condition itself. We had many, but I particularly treasure the memory of the one who cheered my efforts on with a cry of "Good on ya, mate!" Australian by birth, Nola Maureen Flanagan Shirley ("that's my name; use all of it!") was one of the most influential people in Bryce's life. We met Nola back in Chapter One; she was Bryce's paraeducator for three years. After that she became a member of our family and I of hers. Her relationship with Bryce was pure karma: they arrived at Capitol Hill School on the same day in 1997, both assigned to a new developmental kindergarten classroom. They left on the same day in 2004, she to retirement and he to middle school. We stood on the sidewalk in front of the school, together there for the last time on an afternoon in June and I thought, *He looks so grown up since that first day, and she looks exactly the same to me. How does that work?* No time to ponder; he's flying down the walk, shirttails aloft on the breeze. He's not running away from us; he's rushing delightedly, confidently, to discover the next phase of his life.

During the years Nola guided Bryce, she wrote to me every day in a school-home communication notebook, so I thought I had a good picture of what daily life in the classroom was like for Bryce. Some years later, with the perspective of hindsight, I became more and more curious about the minute-by-minute construction of the foundation she'd built under him. During a long conversation on her homey back deck, I asked her how it was that she'd been so successful with Bryce. "That's pretty simple," she said. "He trusted me."

That's pretty simple. He trusted me.

Doesn't that come close to being oxymoronic? It's an uncomplicated statement, but for most people, trust is surely one of the most complex and risk-laden of human relationships. For someone with autism, it's even more so. How had Nola built that trust?

Her reply: "Bryce trusted us because we didn't tell him he had to do something—we showed him what good things could happen if he did." He learned that doing what was asked of him had consequences he would enjoy. "And I never asked him to do something I wasn't doing myself," she added. "Whether it was mixing finger paints, going to Field Day, or cleaning up the science experiment, adult and child, we did it together."

> **"He trusted us because we didn't tell him he had to do something—we showed him what good things could happen if he did."**

Time and again throughout the morning on that sunny porch, our conversation boomeranged back to that core of trust. And boomerang is the proper metaphor, an Australian tool "designed to return to the person who throws it," according to the dictionary. What was that boomerang gathering on its journeys before it elliptically returned to her?

108

Respect.

The bricks of Bryce's trust in Nola were composed of her uncompromising respect for him and the way he saw the world. Each demonstration of respect strengthened the team foundation under them. The result was a self-confident child who was able to venture out of that world of self, attempt new experiences, rise to social and academic challenges, and take calculated risks despite the obstacles his autism presented. Bryce's day was a roadmap guided by Nola's respect for his need for:

- Predictability and routine

- Feeling like he had a choice, not backed into a corner, put on the spot or dictated to

- Visual cueing

- Personal space and accommodation of his tactile defensiveness and other sensory issues that interfered with learning

Trust is the foundation of learning, not an add-on.

- Extra time to acclimate to or prepare for a potentially difficult task or activity

Our student with autism likely knows nothing of French philosophy or Rene Descartes' "I think, therefore I am." But if he could paraphrase, he might say:

I trust, therefore I can.

Trust is the foundation of learning, not an add-on. Your autistic student must interact hour-by-hour with a world that most often doesn't understand his way of thinking and processing, his actions and reactions. It's likely he's already lost the childhood naivete that allows most non-autistic children to trust authority figures without much question. Chances are he's already had more than a few run-ins with adults who, in the words of Jennifer McIlwee Myers, "attempt to use humiliation or public embarrassment to 'teach us a lesson.' We get way too much of that. The only lesson learned is that we can't trust you."

An unconscionable amount of contemporary education is predicated on measurable units of academic knowledge. It's too easy to lose track of the immeasurables, the invaluable building blocks of not only trust, but respect, acceptance, and kindness. These form the foundation under not only successful learning, but successful living. The construction of those measurable units of academic knowledge on top of this foundation shouldn't displace it or even take precedence over it.

Jennifer, who gave us an unflinching look at a teacher whose inflexible attitude engendered loathing rather than learning, gives us an opposite but equally startling child's perspective on a teacher who gained her trust and made an enormous impact in her life:

> Our class was in the school library, and we were supposed to be working on our reports. I, however, was just about bouncing off the walls. With all the kids working independently, the library was way too chaotic for me to "settle down."

> This must have been the umpteenth time that my library behavior had been hyper and inappropriate. My teacher, Mr. Rhine, asked me to step out into the hall with him. Then he did something remarkable.

First, he explained that my behavior was distracting and irritating to the other students, and it would be good if I could not bother them while they were working. *I did not know this until he told me.* Then he told me that he knew I was very capable of writing the report, but he also knew that I genuinely couldn't settle down and was unable to study in the library with the other students. And then he asked me, what could he do to help me? What did I need to be able to do the work?

I genuinely didn't know. I just knew that whenever we had to all work "independently," I went nuts. I couldn't think of what to tell him.

It didn't matter that I didn't know what to ask for. What mattered to me was that instead of yelling or scolding, he admitted that he didn't understand why I behaved as I did and didn't know how to help me.

After years and years of being told I was purposely being a problem, that I was unmotivated and an underachiever, to have a teacher finally admit he just didn't understand what was going on was the most wonderful thing in the world.

He was honest instead of arrogant. Instead of projecting laziness and lack of motivation onto my actions, he admitted his confusion. Since I was confused about my own behavior, too, I could relate and understood his distress.

111

I never did figure out what to ask him for, but it didn't matter. *I would have crawled through broken glass for that man.* He actually cared and he didn't vilify me for behaviors I couldn't control. I still had lots of problems at school, but I did my best for him.

My "problem" behaviors were and had always been about social cluelessness, sensory issues, and huge amounts of anxiety and fear. Most teachers added to my anxiety, fear, and misery by labeling me and stressing me out with their hostile assumptions. Mr. Rhine didn't do that. He was the best teacher I ever had.

Like Jennifer, I too learned early on that an honest "I don't understand why he does this—but let's try to find out" was a lot more constructive than "He could do it if he wanted to." The first response arises out of respect and a willingness to learn, the second out of arrogance, a fundamental lack of understanding of autism spectrum disorders, and a fatal lack of curiosity. It's the difference between "This kid is giving me a hard time. How can I get him to stop?" and "This child is having a hard time. How can I help him?"

Here's an example: I cringe every time I hear an adult, whether parent or teacher, tell me that this child shouldn't get special treatment because it wouldn't be fair to the rest of the class or the rest of the family. First of all, accommodation based on neurological need isn't special treatment. Are we extending special treatment to the child who must wear glasses to see? Secondly, the concept of "fair" as so many adults conceive it is a trap when applied to the child with autism. This explanation of "fair" in my book *Ten Things Every Child with Autism Wishes You Knew* is one for which readers often thank me:

"Fair" is one of those hazy, imprecise terms that can be very perplexing to our child. He doesn't think in terms of fair or unfair but does know he's having trouble balancing his needs with the rules. As parents, teachers, or coaches, we generally think of "fair" as meaning impartial, even-handed, equitable, unbiased. Family rules, school rules, team rules apply to each sibling, student or teammate equally. But autism "un-levels" the playing field. It pot-holes the field. All things are *not* being equal. So our thinking on the subject of "fair" must change. Here it is:

"Fair" does not mean everything is absolutely equal.

"Fair" is when everyone gets what they need.

A popular internet graphic illustrates this in inarguable fashion. Three children are watching a baseball game from behind a fence. One child is tall enough to see over the fence without assistance. The other two are not. One is given a small box to stand on. The smallest child is given a large box to stand on. Now all three can see over the fence. They didn't get the same treatment, but what they got made it possible for all to experience the game equally. What each got was fair.

Take a hard look in the mirror on this one. If we're honest with ourselves, "no special treatment" is sometimes a cover-up for, frankly, laziness on our part or an unwillingness to acknowledge that we don't know what to do. And sometimes it's just plain mean. I once heard of a mom who refused to divide her batch of cookie dough into two parts, one with nuts and one without, because she "won't cater to" her autistic son. He's told her that nuts feel like rocks in his mouth and he's afraid to bite down on them, but nuts in cookies suits her, and if he wants a cookie badly enough, he'll eat them with nuts. He has to learn that he can't have things his way—it's her way or no way. No "special treatment" for her son!

If every moment is a learning moment, what did this child learn to expect from this mother?

Whether or not one mom can accommodate a legitimate sensory-based preference is a microcosm for the whole issue of empowering our autistic student by respecting his differences, developing his ability to make choices and get needs met in a positive manner. Absent those relationship dynamics, trust can't grow. Making good choices is a make-or-break life skill. The child with autism must develop this skill the same as any other child, but for him, he has a distance to travel before even arriving at the starting line. Effective decision-making skills can only be taught in an atmosphere of trust and empowerment. And like any other skill, competence comes only with practice, and lots of it. Our student might hold out this advice:

Offer me real choices—and only real choices.

- Don't offer me a choice or ask a "Do you want...?" question unless you're willing to accept no for an answer. "No" may be my honest answer to "Do you want to read out loud now?" or "Would you like to partner with William for science lab?" It's hard for me to trust you when the choices you offer aren't true choices.

  You take for granted the number of choices you have on a daily basis. You constantly choose one option over others knowing that having choices and being able to choose gives you control over your life. For me, choices are much more limited, which is why it can be harder to feel confident about myself. Give me opportunities for choice whenever you can, so I can practice making decisions and become more involved in the activities, people, and world around me.

- If you can change a "have-to" to a choice, I can learn faster. It can be as simple as, instead of saying "Write your name and the date the top of the page," say "Would you like to write your name first, or would you like to write the date first?" or "Which would you like to write first, letters or numbers?"

- Keep your end of the agreement once I've made a choice. Changing fifteen minutes of computer time to five because you're running late, or changing the choice in the middle of an activity (like saying "Oh, look, let's do this instead.") dampens my trust in you. In my concrete autism way of thinking, a deal is a deal. That goes for both of us.

- Giving me choices helps me learn, but I also need to understand that there will be times when you can't. When this happens, I won't get as frustrated if I understand why:

  - "I can't give you a choice in this situation because it's dangerous. You might get hurt."

  - "I can't give you that choice because it would be bad for Danny (have a negative effect on another child)."

  - "I give you lots of choices, but this time it needs to be an adult choice."

This time it needs to be an adult choice. Will we choose to invest the effort in building trust as a precursor to learning and expectation? Will we respect and honor the verbal and behavioral feedback we get from our autistic student as legitimate and valid, and act upon

115

it accordingly? Will we recognize that if we decline to choose, that in fact becomes the choice? Teachers, I can't give you that choice because it would be bad for Danny!

How about this for our new motto: In trust we trust.

Can I trust you?

Chapter Nine

Believe

I began writing this chapter as an exploration of what it means to believe in a child, to instill and nurture an attitude of confident can-do in a student, and in ourselves as teacher-adults. It's still about that, but the autistic adult community has spoken out more loudly in recent years, a message that society's general failure to believe them when they **Long before an autistic child understands what you mean by "I believe in you," they will understand and need to hear, "I believe you."** relate their experiences about being autistic is a major obstacle to their being able to fully integrate with community as their authentic, capable, valuable, and productive selves.

Long before an autistic child understands what you mean by "I believe in you," they will understand and need to hear, "I believe you."

One of the most poignant stories ever told in one of my round table groups came from a grandmother whose grandson had been sent home from school for "behavior" and refused to talk to his mother or anyone but Grandma. Why? Because, he told her, "No one wistens to me. No one bewieves me." He'd tried to communicate that he'd been bullied. When no one stepped up to help, he retaliated in kind. He, not the abuser, had been punished for his behavior. His grandmother called that day A Lesson in Listen for all concerned.

So many autistic children and adults say that one of the most difficult aspects of their autism is that "no one bewieves" them. Whether it's sensory issues, social situations, or motor or cognitive challenges, too often the response is denial.

It's yucky.
No, it's not; it's good for you.

I don't get it. I don't know how to do this.
Try harder.

I don't understand what you're saying.
Look me in the eye and listen up!

It's too bright/too loud/too creepy/too cold.
No, it's not, so buck up (suck it up, straighten up, chin up).

As the child in the story above so deftly illustrated, believing that our perspective is the only believable one is a surefire way to ensure that meaningful communication, problem solving, and learning won't happen.

If you've ever started a sentence with "Believe me…" (and who among us hasn't?), it shouldn't be hard to put yourself in the shoes of a child who wants to be believed but can't take for granted, as many of us do, that she will be. "Never underestimate the power and influence of validating a child," wrote one of my Facebook readers who grew up to be an educator. "I went to three different schools in first grade because I had a mother who believed me and fought to find the right environment for me."

But another reader expressed reluctance about wholesale believing autistic children because they don't always communicate "authentically." True that may be sometimes, but learning to communicate authentically (a subjective word) is a lifelong process of constant refinement, autistic or not. We have to start by instilling in the child that we will listen respectfully to whatever manner in which they wish to communicate, and then proceed from there. If a child told me he rode a unicorn to school, I would never say, "No, you didn't. Unicorns aren't real." I would say, "Wow, I've never seen a unicorn. I'm curious—tell me more!" Then I would listen and follow up with the exploratory questions that would help me understand what he's trying to communicate and why in this manner. Indirect communication doesn't necessarily equate to inauthenticity.

The scars of not believing our children can last a lifetime. From a distance of many decades, Jennifer McIlwee Myers relates her early elementary school experience:

> The weird (and incredibly frustrating) thing to me was that teachers would refuse to believe me when I really had no reason to lie and wasn't doing anything wrong. In second grade health class, we were taught that we needed to swallow our food before taking a drink to avoid choking (????). I told the teacher privately that I couldn't do it. I just could not successfully swallow food without taking a slug of liquid to wash it down.
>
> Her response? "Oh, I think you can. I think you need to try a little harder."

I still can't eat without using a beverage to wash down every bite. Never could. And I could never convince that teacher that I wasn't lying to her or being lazy. She was the most popular teacher in the school, both with students and teachers. All her students, including me, adored her. But she couldn't accept oral-motor differences as a possibility. Nor would she believe sensory issues were real.

That was the year I learned that there was literally no adult I could trust or lean on. Over and over I found that every single one believed they knew what I thought, felt, and experienced better than I did and simply dismissed anything I said to the contrary. Being autistic meant living in a world of constant de facto gaslighting.

It wasn't so much a power struggle as an inability to understand that people vary from each other in weird and wild ways. It's the same as when I told her that sometimes I couldn't hear or see her when I was reading (because of hyperfocus) and she didn't believe me. Then again, teachers generally got upset that I "stubbornly ignored them" when I got absorbed in stuff. They just didn't have enough imagination to get it.

The threshold from believing your student to believing in them isn't always a definitive line, but it does exist for every child regardless of ability or position in life. Actress Reese Witherspoon looked dazzling in her vintage beaded Dior gown when she accepted her 2005 Academy Award for Best Actress. Her acceptance speech should also achieve vintage status: "I am so blessed to have my... mother and father here. And I just want to say thank you so much for everything, for being so proud of me. It didn't matter if I was making my bed or making a movie. They never hesitated to say how proud they were of me. And that means so very much to a child."

I believe in believing. Nearly all children, whatever their abilities, have the potential to achieve more than what societal stereotypes may suggest, and nearly all children have the ability to do more than they're capable of today. In helping them build a belief in themselves, that's the measuring stick that matters most. That's why, when you **When you lapse into thinking of all the things this child can't do, remember to add one of the most powerful words we have: "yet."** lapse into thinking of all the things this child can't do, remember to add one of the most powerful words we have: "yet." It's as simple as asking ourselves, what is this child doing now that they weren't able to do last year at this time?

In the previous chapter we talked about trust being the foundation of the teacher-student relationship. The fast-lane to building that trust is to nurture and communicate your belief that this child is capable, of learning, doing, and becoming.

Numerous autistic adults have told me that, as children, they could sense far more than they could communicate, and the number one thing they could sense was whether or not an adult thought they "could do it." Expecting too little was as discouraging as expecting too much. The ones who will go the furthest, they say, are the ones whose teachers believe that autism imposes no inherent upper limits other than their own willingness to stretch as a teacher, and who know that they must lead, not merely point, the way toward the far reaches of a student's potential.

121

Like learning, like behavior, like communication and trust, belief is circular. It goes both ways, all ways. And for better or worse, according to the actions you choose, it's contagious. When you communicate your unfettered belief to your child or student, you encourage him to believe in you as well. That belief in you is what gives him the courage and the impetus to try unfamiliar experiences, a deeply difficult step for many autistic kids. For us, it was a long march requiring relentless patience, but Bryce did finally arrive at a place where he believed in me enough to approach new things, trusting that I wouldn't send him into a situation where he had little chance of success or enjoyment.

Adopting a true belief in your student shouldn't be that hard, given the human race's long-standing willingness to believe in that which they can't actually see yet. Most major religions are based upon such faith, and literature is filled with such moments. Who among us ever experienced *Peter Pan* without being drawn into the plight of Tinkerbell, who will die unless we believe in her? In the memorable musical *The King and I*, the king soundly berates his children, raised in tropical Siam, for not believing Mrs. Anna's description of snow. She tries to smooth the moment over by reminding him that they've never actually seen snow. "Never seen?" he booms. "If they believe only what they see, why do we have school?" Indeed!

My path to achieving True Believer status began with a teacher: Sarah, the adapted PE teacher you met in Chapter Six. Sarah went so many extra miles with Bryce as to constitute a marathon, but her most striking achievement was to teach him to ride a two-wheel bike. I had struggled for two years trying to teach him. "I will teach him," she said. "I will do it on my lunch hour." We brought his bike to school and kept it in a locked equipment closet in the gym. It took her less than forty-five minutes, three fifteen-minute sessions. In a conversation several years later, I asked Sarah if Bryce's learning experience with the bike was typical for an autistic child.

"Don't know," she said. "Bryce is the first. Actually, only."

"First and only *what*?" I asked, puzzled.

"First and only child with autism I ever taught to ride a bike."

"No!" I said, not able to *believe* it. "Where are the rest of them?"

"They're not riding bikes."

Back she went into her mantra about belief. "It wasn't about the bike. You believed that Bryce could do it and instilled that belief in him," she said. "He wanted to do it for himself, but he also wanted to do it for you. Not all parents and teachers have that faith in the child, and the child feels that."

She talked to me for an hour that day, and although she was a PE teacher, very little of what she said was about physical ability or motor skills. "Every kid I've ever worked with has an innate sense of whether the adults in their life believe they can do it," she told me. A few half-hour sessions a week with a specialist can only supplement, not compensate for, a belief system at home and in the classroom.

There are many reasons why teachers and parents-as-teachers may lose traction on the road to belief. Sometimes it's a matter of being misinformed or uninformed about autism and about the potential in autistic kids. But one reason I hear with startling frequency is that both parents and professionals get stuck in a grief process, unable to form an honest understanding of the range of a child's disability while also recognizing the child's strengths. We may not call it grief, it may not look or feel like typical grief, and we may not even be aware of it. But that's exactly what it is if we:

- cap our expectations with thoughts like, "he'll never do that."

- cling to our disappointment over what we think he'll never do instead of celebrating the things at which he's terrific, and encouraging them whole-heartedly

- feel ashamed of or impatient with the behaviors and habits of the child that may look odd to the non-autistic world

- persist in the idea that the child is choosing to be belligerent, lazy, or withdrawn, rather than acknowledging that he thinks and experiences his physical and social environment differently, and confronting the complex work of ferreting out sensory, environmental, or biochemical triggers.

Grief is always about loss, and it isn't limited to personal relationships; it can apply to professional losses and perceived failures as well. Depression, denial, and anger are all part of the grief process, and it's natural that we may either consciously or unconsciously retreat from that which feels like failure. Whether we are a teacher or parent, it's hard to admit these things about ourselves. But it's the first step to liberating ourselves from them.

Sarah's formula for success works with any kind of learning:
Repetition breeds familiarity.
Familiarity breeds confidence.
Confidence brings belief.
Belief brings action.

Whether you call it ability, disability, or different ability, it's only part of the picture. The seeds of a child's success rest in you. Here are five important things you can do to instill belief in your autistic student.

1. Beyond merely believing in your student, to act on that belief is what makes things happen. Actively seek out and place him in situations where he will experience success. Look for opportunities where she can lead in a comfortable way, or offer important support functions at things she's good at, such as behind-the-scenes organizing tasks for a school event or reading a favorite book to a younger class. Remember Jennifer McIlwee Myers' story about the teacher who refused to capitalize on her interest in dictionaries? That was an opportunity lost, taken to a shameful degree.

2. If you're a parent, you're a teacher, too. Involve yourself. "Don't fall into a pass-your-kid-off mentality, whether it's six hours a day in school or forty-five minutes in an after-school activity," Sarah says. Play with your child, take her places, read with and to her. Watch how she does things; try to see how she learns and where she needs help. Work out how you can break down challenging tasks into smaller pieces for her. *Be curious about her.*

3. Involve family, friends, people at school—everyone in the child's world. The more reinforcement a child has, the more he'll progress and the more he'll let others in. Bryce was surprised, then delighted, when his teachers attended his swim meets and community theatre performances. Two of his friends joined his baseball team after hearing about it from us.

4. Allow your student or child to be who she is—which may not be what you expect. It bears repeating: Where the expectation is too high, it can turn the child off to the very things you desire for her. Where the expectation is too low, gifts and talents go undiscovered.

5. Throw out any growth or developmental milestone lists or charts you get from pediatricians, books, or websites. They're irrelevant to your autistic student. Every child, regardless of ability or disability, is going to grow and develop at his own pace. "It's not about doing it in any specific order or in any specific way," Sarah says. "Children will flourish if they're nurtured and if their way of doing things is celebrated."

As teachers and parent-teachers, what we want for our student can probably be described with a common vocabulary. Positive process and results. Forward movement as well as lateral growth. What we have to ask ourselves is this: in deed and in thought, is what we're doing now moving toward or away from those goals? What do we believe of this child, and will that belief bring us movement that benefits the child, or not? All motion is relative—if we stand still, we'll find that any goals we had for the child or for ourselves as professionals and parents will move further and further away.

Somewhere in my own long-ago adventures as an elementary school student, a teacher gave me a copy of Walter Wintle's children's poem "Thinking," which begins:

> If you think you're beaten, you are.
> If you think you dare not, you don't.
> If you'd like to win, but you think you can't,
> It's almost a cinch you won't.

Some might consider the poem trite by today's standards, but I was a child, and it resonated with me (even back then, I automatically substituted "woman" for "man" in my mind). It started bubbling to the surface of my consciousness more frequently once I had children, and especially once I realized that my children would face a steeper uphill climb in life than most. I came to appreciate how powerful a qualifier that little word *if* was. But the choice was mine whether it would be one of constraint—as in *ifs*, *ands*, and *buts*—or one of possibility, as in Wintle's poem.

You don't have to call it belief. You can call it conviction, positivity, or self-fulfilling prophecy. You can call it anything you want. But in today's over-hyped, ultra-competitive, measured-to-a-gnat's-eye, take-everything-to-the-next-level, give-everything-a-score, must-do-must-have society, I had to give my sons something more real, more lasting, something that would give them roots during our time together and at the same time give them wings when the time came for them to venture out on their own—whether for an hour, a week, or a lifetime. As my teacher had done thirty-five years earlier, I gave them Wintle's poem:

Life's battles don't always go to the stronger or faster man.
Sooner or later, the one who wins is the one who thinks he can.

Chapter Ten

Teach Me "How to Fish"

See me as a capable adult and hold that vision.

One of the luckiest breaks I ever caught was the school district geography that landed us with Teacher Christine as Bryce's first special educator. Even before my head stopped spinning from the initial identification of autism, even before I began to learn what autism was, she told me clearly all the things that autism wasn't: it wasn't shameful, wasn't a prison sentence, nor was it a reflection on my parenting, and above all, it wasn't a stereotype. "They're not headbangers," she said. "They're some of the coolest kids I know. It might hurt to hear the word *autism* or *autistic* applied to your child; I understand that. But the label is the means to the services. You want the services, because he's a potentially independent adult."

A *potentially independent adult.*

With those three little words, I knew what my long-range goal was: to leave this planet knowing that Bryce would be okay without me.

The old Chinese proverb came to mind: "Give a man a fish and your feed him for a day. Teach him to fish and you feed him for a lifetime."

I'd have to teach my son to fish. It would require far more of me than leading him to the allegorical river and throwing the line in the water. Just as he had to walk before he ran, he would need to become an independent student, child, and teen before he could become a self-sufficient adult.

The road to independent adulthood starts with our teaching our student or child to handle independently as much of his "day job"— being a student—as possible, instilling the habits and skills that allow him to do as much for himself as possible, with *patient instruction* from teachers and parents.

That directive is worth dissecting. *Patient*: because your autistic student may require countless repetitions of a skill before becoming competent at it. And he has two strikes against him because, unlike his peers, he may have far fewer opportunities to practice those skills. It's our responsibility as teachers and as parent-teachers to create the additional opportunities he needs, and moreover, to maintain patience through the process, however long it may be. *Instruction*: instructing and guiding, not intercepting and doing it for him in the name of helping, because the goal is that he'll do it himself. And implicit in the responsibility to instruct is that we do it in a manner appropriate to his learning style.

The importance of promoting independence can hardly be over-stated. Many teachers are parents themselves; they understand the time-stress continuum most families function within. But whether it's homework or personal organization, expedience in the moment will impede your student from learning to be independent in the long run. If you pack and unpack his backpack for him every day, how will he learn the importance of being organized, knowing where things are when they are needed, how to find items or information? The same applies to putting together his lunch, completing the last two math problems, leaving the house on time, or zipping his own jacket. I'm a mother and I do understand that sometimes in the morning or evening time crunch, it seems quicker to do it for him. But learning to organize his work and his time, being able to manage his own self-care, clothes, schedule, and money, and learning to use all manner of implements are the skills that will bring him autonomy, and he will only learn them through persistent repetition.

Teach Relevance

Our autistic student would probably tell you that math problems presented without any context don't seem to have a purpose. She asks, I wonder…how is this skill useful to me? Does it teach me whether or not I have enough money for groceries today, and what's the difference between a teaspoon and a tablespoon if I want to make a cake? Why do I need to know how to spell "exponential" on a word list without knowing what it means? I need to know words that help me get things I need or want. So what if I can find Estonia on a map of the world? I need to be able to find the library on a map of my city.

Even in our outstanding school, there were moments when I nearly wept with frustration at the utter irrelevance of how the curriculum was being applied to my son. In elementary school, Bryce was given beginner-level instruction in doing internet research. I was excited to hear about it until I saw the practice worksheet. He'd been assigned to look up things like who won the Grammy for Best Female Singer the year he was born, and what year Spain and Portugal had signed the Treaty of Tordesillas. Neither of these pieces of information had any relevance whatsoever to him. You can imagine the effect on his interest in learning this skill (that seems akin to breathing today but wasn't then): flatter than day-old root beer. Without the ability to generalize the skill (Chapter Three in action), many lost months went by before he became aware that the internet was a great source for information that both interested and helped him. The point of the original lesson had been to introduce a computer skill. How little effort it would have taken to modify that assignment to have him look up something either functional or relevant to him, such as which local parks have bike paths, what the weather was going to be that weekend, or a biography of a favorite author. *Functional!* was my mantra at IEP meetings. I want *functional!* Which, not coincidentally, includes the word *fun*.

And fun is indeed the beginnings of functional. All children, including your autistic student, learn more eagerly through fun. Fun is the doorway to exploration, exploration is the doorway to motivation, and motivation is key to learning. The common ingredient to both fun and motivation is relevance. On the road to independence, your student will learn any skill more quickly if, and possibly only if, you make it relevant to his life and interests. Think of yourself in your own work and how deeply you resent busywork, unnecessary tasks, tedious meetings. With finite energy and time, all of us want our efforts to be applicable to our goals. Your autistic student is no different.

We have now spent a whole book discussing how children with autism think, process, and experience the physical and social world around them. But in coming to a clearer understanding of them, we remind ourselves again that this whole child will develop in many ways common to more typically-developing non-autistic kids. The need for independent living skills is universal among all of us who want to live self-sufficiently as adults, and the fact that a child has autism doesn't release us from our obligation to teach those skills. It does dictate that those skills be taught in a manner understandable to the child's autism way of thinking.

We identify and remove the sensory and environmental barriers to learning, we teach in language appropriate and comprehensible to them, we break large tasks into smaller pieces. We teach them to be functional within their autism—not to replicate "typical" children. Jennifer McIlwee Myers advises, "Please don't try to make us 'normal.' We'd much rather be functional. It's hard to be functional when you have to spend all your time and energy focusing on not tapping your feet." To be accepted, valued, comfortable, and happy with themselves is as much the birthright of the autistic child as it is any other person's.

We teach the indispensable intangibles, like being a friend to have a friend. We teach that no one is perfect, that "mistake" is another word for "let's try again." We guide our children to understanding that no one is a mind-reader and that asking questions is not only a means of getting information, but a means to connecting with people as well.

> **Teach your student to be functional within their autism, not replicate "typical" children. To be accepted, valued, and comfortable with themselves is as much the birthright of the autistic child as it is any other person's.**

We teach the intangibles knowing that the light-bulb moment may not in fact be a moment but more like a sunrise—a slow but rosy dawning of awareness. We trust in the (possibly imperceptible) process of progression that will get us there.

Then we let go. In carefully planned and staged increments, one-step-at-a-time "confidence bricks" on that road to adulthood.

Teach Self-Reliance

Teach me what self-reliance is and the wide range of possibilities it brings me, our student might say. Show me how becoming a do-it-myself person—learning to fish—builds the confidence to know that I can succeed in new situations, be among all kinds of people, and understand that challenges can be hard work, but also worthwhile and fun. I want this, even if I appear fearful of it at the outset. If I don't learn to be self-reliant, I'll always be dependent on you or someone else, and I can see that drags both of us down.

Many educators are familiar with the term "scaffolding" as it relates to teaching. Metaphorically, it's not unlike its concrete definition in the construction industry—the temporary structure that supports workers while a permanent building is under construction. When the permanent structure is complete and support no longer needed, the scaffolding is removed. Scaffolding can range from simple to elaborate, and its removal may happen in stages. But the end result is the same: a standalone structure.

Scaffolding as an educational strategy is the same, and it is particularly useful for developing self-sufficiency in a student with autism. We teach and we up the challenges one level at a time; we remove the supports as each new level of self-reliance is achieved. Removing the support—letting go—is a process, not an event, for both the student and the teacher.

An essential part of the journey toward self-sufficiency is learning to deal with adversity. Accepting our innate fallibility as human beings is a tall order for many people. But for autistic students, it's an even more towering challenge because mistakes may only come in two sizes: nonexistent or crushing. Use scaffolding not just in teaching and building, but in allowing for incremental failure. We must set the stage for little mistakes that lead to the child's ability to handle increasingly larger misfortunes.

From my early days as a mother, I've carried with me this story from a psychologist who spent an afternoon observing a group of toddlers playing at the park, noting that the mothers fell into two groups: the "Kaboom!" mommies and the "Oh no!" mommies. When the fast-moving toddlers would inevitably get ahead of their feet and go splat in the grass or the sawdust, the "Kaboom!" mommies would say "Kaboom!" with smiles and clapping and an "Up you go now!" And the "Kaboom!" kids would do just that. The "Oh no!" mommies would leap up with cries of "Oh no, are you okay?!" and rush to brush off a toddler who often took Mom's reaction as a cue to burst into tears.

Your attitude toward your student is going to be his attitude toward himself. If you can't see him as capable, interesting, and valuable, no amount of education or therapy layered on to top is going to matter.

Attitude is everything. Your attitude toward your student or child is going to be that child's attitude toward himself. If you can't see him and celebrate him as a capable, interesting, productive, and valuable member of the classroom, the family, and the community, no amount of education or therapy layered on top is going to matter.

Teach a man to fish and you feed him for a lifetime.

By teaching our student with autism to fish, we arrive back where we started at the beginning of this book: proof positive that learning is circular. Because the ten things your student wants you to know are the ten things he also needs to know and live to fulfill that vision of a capable, independent adult. He embraces his role as a lifelong learner and teacher. He's connected to others as part of a team—part of many teams as family member, co-worker, neighbor, citizen. He understands and accepts responsibility for his own behavior, and he effectively communicates needs, wants, and information. He understands his own unusual way of thinking and how he must adapt to a world that thinks differently than he does.

He sees himself a whole, brilliantly faceted person—and he likes what he sees. He's curious about his world. He believes in himself. *He* has the vision of a capable, independent adult.

I wonder how far he can go now?

Continuance

"**B**ooks end, but stories don't," Bryce observed while I mulled how to shape the ending of this one. "We're all a never-ending story." So it seems only right that he should be the one to end this book, with his own open-ended story.

He moved on from the stories told in these pages to graduate from high school as valedictorian, his adviser calling him "humble and classy...his heart could easily fill this auditorium." He completed several college credentials and successfully transitioned to the workplace where, though he notes "it's not easy being autistic," he now has a long record as an exemplary employee. Early in his college years, he wrote an essay for a course final—in pencil and in less than ninety minutes—that spoke to a deep truth about growing up autistic, and the make-or-break role we all play in guiding a child to meeting their unique full potential. It appeared, to heartfelt response, in several publications, and it's a joy to be able to close this book's circle of learning by including it here.

I Choose to Be Optimistic

by Bryce Notbohm

During the years I was growing up, I developed the sense that if I'm doing a task that's challenging, I should always try to take things the simple way. The simple way involves patience; it means being hardworking but avoiding unnecessary complications. This gives me the strength to believe that things will turn out all right for me once the task is completed. If I took what I consider to be the hard way, pushing myself to try to, say, do and be things that I'm not—such as be an extroverted person, when I'm more introverted—it would be much more stressful. Maybe things wouldn't have turned out to be as positive as I hoped, maybe I wouldn't have been as successful as I've been able to be, had I worried too much about the worst that could happen. Having a little faith in yourself and others is important. No matter what faith might look like to you, what matters is that you're able to see what you look like inside yourself—what makes you, you.

My parents always gave me confidence in myself. I chose to stick with it even when, as I grew older, I became aware that other families were different and I sometimes felt I didn't fit in with others. I stuck with it anyway because it's how I was raised and I never would want to give up the things that I saw in life first. The time I spent growing up with my parents, my brother, my grandparents, my aunts and uncles, my cousins, and many excellent teachers convinced me to become someone who could see the world as it should be. I call it "noble optimism," and it is what I am destined to be for as long as I live.

In middle school, my maturity was emerging but the people surrounding me seemed like they lived in a more complex environment. I didn't feel I belonged there. I was concerned that my generation was becoming a rude one. But I still didn't let my faith in myself fly away.

I attended an outstanding high school for students with learning differences. There, I got to know classmates who were not only people with different skills, but whose struggle in life was similar to mine. We learned that what was being taught wasn't just random knowledge being fed into our heads but how it would help us succeed and get through life a lot better. The power I developed was a strength that I likely wouldn't have experienced at a larger, more typical high school. It's a pity this kind of personalized education and the mental discipline it teaches isn't available at all schools, around the world, whether or not a student has a learning difference. When we graduated, our teachers wrote each of us personal notes like this one: "You will face challenges and battles, you will meet failures and successes. It's part of life. Don't be dismayed. *You will make it.* I have every confidence in you. It's only the beginning, and you're in control. *You will make it.*"

Now in my college years, twenty years into the process of growing into an independent adult, I feel like I've arrived at a much harder step. My emotions have become more intense than they were when I was little, but I have never given up my beliefs. The intensity of my emotions doesn't make me feel aggressive, but allows me to show assertive confidence in my self-advocacy, standing up for myself better than I did long ago. I feel like I can make my own decisions about how I can best handle my life. Stress is an enemy that's still on the run; like everyone else, I have stress and it affects me, but now I feel I can defeat it next time it returns. In envisioning my life going forward, the choice that I've clarified is something that not only my folks taught me but I've learned for myself as I've gotten older. It's a technique that might falter sometimes in a predicament but the way it makes my heart feel and how it motivates me is why I choose it.

This is what I've had all along. I choose to be optimistic.

— December 2012

Questions and prompts for discussion, self-reflection, or self-expression

How to use these questions and prompts

Throughout the book, you've been asked to consider perspectives, language, structures, and patterns that may not be familiar to you, that may fall outside so-called standards for teaching, for how to think about being a teacher. Circular learning, the classroom community, defining what it means to give a child functional language, the reciprocity of their behavior and yours, the role of trust, curiosity, and scaffolding in education—integrating these concepts into your teaching persona requires something more creative, more expansive than the usual kind of group discussion, although such interactions can certainly be useful.

These questions and prompts invite many and varied ways to explore, from private for-your-eyes-only to those larger-forum discussions. The aim of these questions and prompts is to guide you to examine perspectives you may not yet have discovered, to challenge ones you hold close and perhaps thought were unshakeable, and to solidify those which define and embody you. For me, that was the most wondrous part of being the parent-teacher of an autistic child: the discovery of perspectives so far outside my own, the wonder of it, and how it led to my seeking and deeply considering the perspectives of others in everything I do. It has allowed me to temper my negative feelings without erasing them (some things in this world are worthy of our anger and intense dislike) and frame them more constructively. So, if some of these questions and prompts make you uncomfortable (or exasperated or angry), consider the value of approaching the issue from an opposite perspective.

No charts, games, or instructions for teaching materials here. Some of the prompts call for a specific action such as making a list or actively making observations, but some are intentionally vague. They can be interpreted either literally or figuratively, in a concrete sense or an emotional one. Perhaps you'll challenge yourself to answer both ways, at different times. Some questions or prompts may confuse or discomfit you, or they may excite and motivate you. It can also be insightful to return to such prompts after a passage of some time, a few months or a year or two, and see how your perspective has changed.

THINK. No need to write; go paperless, go screenless. Batteries not included or needed. No spelling or grammar check. Perspective can develop in eloquent, evocative ways without ever writing a word. It takes courage to be alone with your thoughts. Paper can be easily destroyed, but not so the energy of thought.

WRITE. If the written word is your medium, the wonderful thing is that what you write can remain a work in progress for as long as you want it to, growing, changing, moving through its own seasons, spawning offshoots.

DISCUSS. The prompts in this book can be useful as opening points of a discussion, with a partner, colleague, friend, or family member or within a group. If at all possible, seek out autistic adults for their firsthand insights.

OTHER MEDIUMS. Drawing, painting, and many art mediums are the most meaningful forms of expression for some people. The artwork for the covers of several foreign editions of my books were done by autistic artists for whom words are not the communication mode of first choice.

Let the exploration begin.

List three ways in which your classroom engages in circular learning. If you can't think of any, has this book prompted you to think about creating opportunities for circular learning? If so, list three things you might try to encourage learning from student to teacher, from student to student, or through other avenues.

*

Are the team dynamics in your school productive, indifferent or poisonous? Why do you think this is? If the team dynamics are less than productive, what might be done to improve them? Brainstorm a list of possible actions you could take, regardless of how likely or unlikely they seem. Share the list in a problem-solving team setting if you can.

*

Do you believe that students bear some responsibility to each other to create an interdependent classroom learning community? Why or why not? What are some obstacles to achieving this? What actions might you take to achieve a wholly inclusive, integrated classroom?

*

Chapter Four suggests that there is no "bad" or "negative" behavior, only behavior as communication, and that only by honest examination of our own adult behavior can we positively impact a child's. This can be painful but revelatory. Think or write about a teaching incident you would like to forget, where perhaps you exhibited "bad" behavior or judgment. Let a day or so go by, and then delve into the incident.

- Why did you behave that way?

- Did you consciously choose it or was it instinctive, reflexive, or reactive?

- How did your student (or coworker or student's parent) react?

- What was achieved? Explore each emotion.

- If you could do it over, what would you change?

- Did you owe the child an apology? If so, did you apologize? If not, why not?

- Did you find resolution or peace?

*

What kinds of sensory accommodations have you made or are you willing to make for your autistic student in your classroom? How have other students reacted to these accommodations?

*

Write a list of every idiom you can think of. Keep a small notebook with you for a day or two and jot down every idiom you hear. Become very aware of how idioms, puns, metaphors, phrasal verbs, and other figurative speech saturate our everyday language. Create a game for the whole class that helps children learn the concrete meanings of idioms.

*

How did the exercise in Chapter Five about removing your mode of functional communication make you feel? What changes might you consider making to the manner in which you communicate with your autistic student?

*

List twenty ways your student with autism is like most other students.

*

Chapter Seven quotes Albert Einstein as saying, "It is a miracle that curiosity survives formal education." What do you think he meant? List five ways this statement might be true in your classroom or school. Then list five ways your classroom does encourage curiosity or what you might do to further encourage curiosity, especially for your autistic students.

*

Create an ongoing classroom activity or display that encourages the *I wonder* mentality.

*

Have you ever actively discussed the role of trust in learning with your students, either individually or as a classroom community? Create a classroom activity wherein students and teachers can come up with examples and share ideas about earning and showing trust in each other.

*

Reflect: Even if only occasionally, do you ever find yourself saying, "Trust me" to a student rather than demonstrating trustworthy traits, such as reliability, consistency, respect, and patience? Do you believe authority figures are owed respect and trust as a result of their position? Think about how this plays out in your own life. How does it make you feel?

*

Envisioning your autistic student as an adult, write an ideal job description for him. Keep in mind that many jobs that might be ideal for him don't yet exist.

*

Write for ten minutes about a time when you told the truth and no one believed you.

*

A high school senior working on a science project once asked me: "Is it possible the reason more and more kids are diagnosed as autistic is because the next generations of our world will need to be autistic so as to survive, like natural evolution?" No one can yet say whether this thoughtful and inquisitive young woman is right or wrong. Discovery of what we don't yet know is the very reason for the exploration of science. But considering the thinking structure of autism and the manner in which autistic students relate socially and experience their physical environment, think, write about, or discuss:

- How would the classroom community experience and that of the school as a whole change if those now considered neurotypical required the assistance of people who think and function as autistic?

- How would it change how you teach?

- Would some of these changes be for the better? Describe why or why not.

- Would it be beneficial to implement some of those changes in your current classroom and school?

- Did this question raise unexpected, possibly conflicting, possibly exciting, emotions in you? How did it make you feel, not only as a teacher, but as a human, as a member of a community, and as a parent if you are one?

- If you are an autistic teacher, would you be comfortable discussing this question with your non-autistic coworkers?

Follow-up questions

Prior to reading this book, what expectations did you have for your autistic student? Did anything in the book change your expectations? How? Did anything reinforce your existing thoughts?

∗

Prior to reading this book, what beliefs did you hold about autism in general? Did anything in the book change your beliefs about autism? How? Did anything reinforce your existing thoughts?

∗

If you were to hand this book to a colleague or parent, which points would you most want to convey?

*

Will your student's life be different as a result of you reading this book? Will yours?

[Follow-up questions adapted from *Ten Things Every Child with Autism Wishes You Knew*, third edition, Ellen Notbohm, 2019]

Acknowledgments

My work on the original edition of this book coincided with my son Connor's last semester of high school, so it was only natural that I spent some time reflecting on the constellation of educators with whom we interacted over the sixteen years of both our sons' educations. I started a list but lost count after 100. Of that 100, three were genuine stinkers, and perhaps a handful were questionable. The rest of them, the bountiful majority, ranged from very good to simply superlative. They ply their excellent work under increasingly difficult, often nigh impossible conditions, and their dedication humbles me. I could never do what they do, and I revere every one of them.

The hearts and minds of so many of those teachers and therapists are embodied in this book. Some I have named in specific passages and some I have not, either because they asked not to be identified or because their ideas are presented as composite with other similar thinkers. Either way, please join me in hoping that all autistic kids get to have educators and service providers like those whose ideas shine throughout this book: Roneete Lynas, Ariel Nadel, Christine Hunt, Jackie Druck, Mary Schunk, Nola Shirley, Veda Nomura, Julieann Barker, Christine Bemrose, Sarah Spella, Patti Rawding-Anderson, to name only a few.

Special thanks to Jennifer McIlwee Myers, author and autism advocate nonpareil, for her clear-eyed and compelling insights into what it's like to navigate life and the education system as a child with an ASD.

Thanks as always to Jennifer Gilpin and the staff of Future Horizons for our relationship, approaching twenty years at this writing, with increasing appreciation every year for the lives we've been honored to touch in every corner of the world.

Veronica Zysk has been my editor since 2003, seven book collaborations now and years of magazine columns in which her unmatchable work and spirit supersede words. The original concept and vision for this book were hers, and I thank her for not accepting less than she knew me to be capable of, particularly when "forceps delivery" of certain chapters became necessary.

My husband Mark has been the anchor supporting all my books, and my son Connor the spark that gave me the confidence to believe in myself as a mother. But without Bryce, there would be no book. As one of my most consequential teachers, wherever he's headed is where I'm going. I wonder where... ?

About the Author

Ellen Notbohm's internationally renowned work has informed and delighted millions in more than twenty-five languages. In addition to her perennial bestseller *Ten Things Every Child with Autism Wishes You Knew*, three other award-winning books on autism, and her widely acclaimed novel *The River by Starlight*, her columns and posts have appeared in major publications and captured audiences on every continent. Ellen's books have won the Chanticleer International Book Awards Grand Prize for Instruction and Insight, Sarton Women's Book Award, Western Writers of American Spur Award, and Independent Publishers Book Awards Gold Medal, been named to the Grand Prize Short List and Montaigne Medal finalist list for the Eric Hoffer Books Awards, and won numerous finalist awards and bookstore staff picks in fiction and nonfiction.

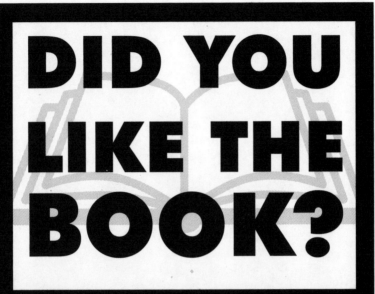

DID YOU LIKE THE BOOK?

Rate it and share your opinion.

amazon.com

BARNES&NOBLE
BOOKSELLERS
www.bn.com

Not what you expected? Tell us!

Most negative reviews occur when the book did not reach expectation. Did the description build any expectations that were not met? Let us know how we can do better.

Please drop us a line at *info@fhautism.com*.
Thank you so much for your support!

One of the autism community's most beloved classics!

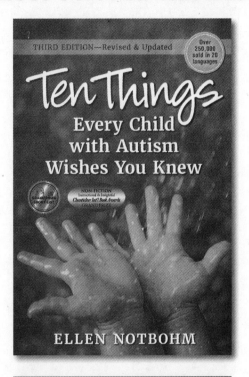

This book offers a one-of-a-kind exploration into how ten core characteristics of autism affect our children's perceptions and reactions to the surrounding physical, sensory, and social environments. The third edition sharpens the focus on these basic aspects while expanding on how our own perspectives shape the life of our child and ourselves, today and for years to come. An all-new section illuminates the breadth of our power of choice and outlines strategies for strong decision-making in every situation.

FUTURE HORIZONS INC.   www.FHautism.com | 817•277•0727